RESOUNDING PRAISE FOR
FLAWLESS!

"Simple, easy-to-read—like looking in the mirror. You'll get the point, and you'll get it quickly—and maybe save a few dollars in therapy!"

—DR. JOYCE L. VEDRAL, author of *Look In, Look Up, Look Out! Be the Person You Were Meant to Be*

"*Flawless!* is good food for the soul."

—FATHER ANGELO SCOLOZZI, Missionaries of Charity 3rd Order

"Dr. Tartaglia jump-starts us toward growth by understanding that character flaws are defensive mechanisms. ('Flaws don't occur because people are bad, but because people are hurting.') He guides us to self-directed change by distinguishing between feats of iron will and the more powerful humility of willingness. *Flawless!* is a powerful, timely guidebook to a healthier, heartier dance through life."

—DR. JIM TUNNEY, former NFL referee and author of *Impartial Judgment*

"*Flawless!* is a must-read from a medical director and an outstanding writer whose decades of working with patients provide him a rich background of understanding human psychology. Dr. Tartaglia is genius at simplifying complex theory into clear, understandable, and practical action steps that will enrich your life and interaction with others."

—PAUL J. MEYER, founder of Success Motivation Institute, Inc., and Leadership Management, Inc.

"Dr. Tartaglia's terrific book *Flawless!* reflects a street-smart and savvy approach that has helped thousands of patients. He is the most knowledgeable psychiatrist I have ever worked with. *Flawless!* is a must-read for anyone bent on turning their life around."

—DAVID TOMA, author of *Turning Your Life Around*

"Dr. Tartaglia has done it! *Flawless!* is a fascinating, realistic, practical guide to happiness. In fact, in a world of illusory promises, his may be the only reliable prescription for peace of mind and contentment. I do know for sure that this prominent psychiatrist has put his finger on exactly the reasons so many bright individuals fall short of the success they are seeking. Fortunately, this book provides us with many inspiring models for success and with the tools that we can use to fix the flaws that are holding us back. Dr. Tartaglia leaves no doubt that we do indeed have the power to change our lives, to create new selves, and to take charge of guiding our own destinies."

—SCOTT DEGARMO, former editor in chief and publisher of *Success* magazine

"Character is crucial in business and in life. In simple language, Louis Tartaglia details flaws we can all identify with, and more importantly, what to do about them."

—THOMAS S. MONAGHAN, founder of Domino's Pizza, Inc.

"*Flawless!* by Dr. Louis Tartaglia is funny, honest, and insightful—much like its author. I enjoyed it immensely and found its practical solutions extremely useful."

—ANNE LINDEN, M.A., director of the New York Training Institute for NLP

"Once again Louis Tartaglia teaches us—at a time when we need reminding—the value of character. In this age of hype and self-promotion, *Flawless!* is a light at our feet that points the way to honesty, tolerance, and greater understanding."

—DENNIS KIMBRO, author of *Think and Grow Rich: A Black Choice*

Flawless!

Flawless!

THE TEN MOST COMMON CHARACTER FLAWS AND WHAT YOU CAN DO ABOUT THEM

Louis A. Tartaglia, M.D.

Eagle  Brook

William Morrow and Company, Inc.

New York

Published by Eagle Brook
An Imprint of William Morrow and Company, Inc.
1350 Avenue of the Americas, New York, N.Y. 10019

Library of Congress Cataloging-in-Publication Data

Tartaglia, Louis A.
Flawless! : The ten most common character flaws and what you
can do about them / by Louis A. Tartaglia.—1st ed.
        p.   cm.
    ISBN 0-688-15609-6 (hardcover : alk. paper)
  1. Characters and characteristics.   2. Personality change.
  3. Change (Psychology)   4. Self-actualization (Psychology)
                    I. Title.
                BF818.T37   1999
158.1—dc21   98-25711
                    CIP

Printed in the United States of America

First Edition

1   2   3   4   5   6   7   8   9   10

BOOK DESIGN BY JENNIFER ANN DADDIO

www.williammorrow.com

To my patients, who taught me how this
"letting go of flaws stuff" really works,
and to my wife, Barbara, who always believed
I could let go of mine even when I had my doubts

ACKNOWLEDGMENTS

There are many avenues of love to the human heart. Every task that has as its outcome an increased love has support from these avenues. I would like to express my gratitude that God has seen to it that these paths to my heart were opened by so many people.

This book started from a chance call on a radio station to say hello to my old buddy Les Brown, "the motivator." During our little session on the air my editor, Joann Davis, happened to be listening. Little did I know it would be such an enlightening experience to work with such an insightful lady. She is perceptive, wise, and has a remarkable understanding of the human condition. Thanks also to Michelle Shinseki, who is kind and always patient with me, even when I talk too much on the phone.

I would also like to thank my agent, Carol Mann, and her staff. Thanks for believing in my work and never giving up the dream.

No acknowledgment would be complete without saying something about the gang at the office. I have to thank all of you, whom I miss terribly: Carol, Linda, Peggy, Donna, and Donna T. You were the best and made life better for a lot of people.

To all my friends who encouraged me to write "your book": Mark Victor Hansen, Jack Canfield, Wayne Dyer, Dave Toma, Robert Schuler, and Father Angelo. Thanks for the support.

And most important to my wife, Barbara, and my five boys, Tony, Anthony, Louis Jr., Dominick, and Dean, you are the best that a husband, father, and stepfather could want. Your love is the finest encouragement that any man could have. You are the reason for believing.

CONTENTS

FOREWORD

It was once said that no man or woman can climb out beyond the limitations of his or her own character. When we look at our leadership, our politicians, our entertainers and sports figures, it becomes crystal clear that we all have the potential to reach great heights. Talent and dogged determination gets you there, but character keeps you there.

In his book *Flawless!* Dr. Lou Tartaglia is taking us into areas of our personality we all need to admit to, acknowledge, examine, and try to improve. Character flaws are something we all have but really don't want to discuss. But in his twenty years of treating patients as a caring and nurturing psychiatrist, Dr. T. has observed and has been a part of countless miracles in his patients' journeys to uncover their greatness and their potential, so that their lives will be more fulfilling and satisfying. Overcoming their individual character flaws has been a large part of these transformations and self-discoveries, resulting in more tranquility and peace in their lives. We are all living in a time of incredible change, and our lives seem like we're racing at breakneck speed toward the twenty-first century. Handling such challenges is much easier if we are comfortable with ourselves and don't feel the need for self-sabotage or the "puffy ego syndrome." However, this involves brutal honesty and continual evaluation of our own character flaws, as well as a commitment to improve these areas of our personalities.

Dr. T. also helps us to recognize and adapt successfully to the flaws of the many other individuals who are near and dear to us, thereby enhancing the quality of our interaction with these important people in our business and personal lives. Our overreactions to the "holes in the soul" of others in our lives can serve to aggravate their problems and their attitudes in general. This book will help to guide us in learning how to soften or modify our response to their character flaws, thereby helping them to work through the difficulties, which will also serve to improve our relationships with such individuals. This is a good example of how we must be willing to do the things today that others will not do, in order to have the things tomorrow (peace of mind, self-fulfillment, good relationships) that others won't have.

Dr. T. has been an important force in my life and career, and I value and trust his ideas. I truly believe that he can help you to re-create yourself, to learn to understand and have more tolerance for the flaws of others, and to live a much happier and fulfilling life! His thoughts are expressed in a very informative and interesting way, so that reading this book is entertaining and enlightening and it doesn't read like a dull textbook. Investing the time and energy in yourself will reap rich rewards for your future success and happiness. In facing our character flaws, we accept the fact that you don't have to be great to get started on this exciting project, but you have to get started to be great!

LES BROWN

CHARACTER FLAWS:

Everybody Has Them

HOW CAN YOU TELL IF YOU ARE POSSESSED BY A FLAW?

Be careful; this is worse than just having the flaw. Here the flaw has you!
Any one of the following may be diagnostic!

1. Do you find yourself "upset" when you need to be calm?
2. Do you lie when it would be better to tell the truth?
3. Would you rather be right even if it wrecks a relationship?
4. Do you hate accepting responsibility and blame others even when you know you are wrong?
5. Does resentment feel like a perfectly normal civil right?
6. Do you worry about things you can't control?
7. Do you fear even when there is nothing to worry about because it feels normal?

8. Are you intolerant of people who are not like you even when you are interested in knowing them?

9. Do you use the excuse that you are a victim whenever it is useful?

10. Do you try to force others to do things your way because you want them to like you?

11. Do you cop out with inadequacy even before you have tried your hardest?

12. Do you love to find fault and share it even when you are aware that it will hurt someone else?

13. Did you graduate from law school or become a politician?

14. Last but most important, do you find yourself using your most common flaw even when you don't want to?

If you're like most of us, you are constantly dealing with people who would rather be right than happy. They are that great class of unfortunate souls who are incapable of admitting they are wrong. They are convinced that their way of living, their way of doing things, is best. These characters wish that the rest of the world would get with their personal program. Then, according to them, everyone would be better off.

Or maybe you have a boss or coworker with a flash-point temper who gets enraged over the silliest things. Some of you might have a spouse or partner who blames you for his or her problems. Do you know anyone who prefers criticism over solutions, or who relishes nurturing resentment? These people have character flaws.

The truth is that everybody has them. Some of us have more than others. You may notice you have them too. I know I have my share. Don't worry if you happen to see your flaws surfacing as I describe them. That is a sign of your own open-mindedness and willingness to get a handle on your problems.

We are a society that is enamored with defective character. We watch thousands of hours of TV and films where the leading role is portrayed by an imperfect character. We watch celebrities, politicians, and stars on and off the screen with an almost morbid fascination for their defects: J. R. on *Dallas,* Jeffrey Geiger on *Chicago Hope,* Diane on *Cheers,* or Abby on *Knots Landing*—the most flawed people seem to be among the most captivating. Perhaps in their struggles we see ourselves.

Great individuals with high character also have glaring faults. It is precisely because they have such high character that their flaws stand out. The common perception that good people have fewer flaws is wrong. It is not a matter of more or fewer flaws. It is the willingness to change them that counts. If you read the lives of saints and sages you will find that they too had to discipline themselves to improve their character. It is in the process of working on your flaws that you develop great strength of character. Strength of character is what this book is about.

Some people, you may have noticed, deliberately cling to their defects of character. In fact there are many who hone their flaws in order to be in control or have power over others. As much as some hate to admit it, there are evil people in this world who use character flaws to get ahead and dominate others. These individuals have always been with us. Our modern, allegedly enlightened society seeks to reform them, even when it is obvious that there is no willingness on their part to change. As a society we have become fascinated with the dark side, like sunbathers who bask in the shadow.

Your Character, Your Reputation

A person's reputation used to be based on living a good and honest life. If you were someone who kept your promises, and didn't take anything you didn't deserve, you were considered good. A man could go to his grave satisfied that he had lived an honest life.

Nowadays a man or woman's reputation is often based on hype, not morality. We judge people by how good they are at doing something. Sports figures are considered great based solely on their performance, not on the kind of people they are. Since most of what goes on in our society is based on promotion, it is publicity and not character that determines our heroes. This constitutes a great moral crisis for our society. Celebrity is revered, and often name recognition is more important than a good name. Worse yet, having a good name no longer implies moral substance. It means visibility through the media. And the media is cultishly devoted to flaws.

In this book you will learn not only how to identify the ten most common character defects but also what to do with them. You may ask, Why bother? I believe that the reward for changing even one of your flaws is greater peace of mind. It is worth it. If you don't think you have any character flaws, feel free to put this book down. You don't need my help. I offer my condolences to your friends and relatives. If you do work on yourself you will learn how to deal with the flaws in others too.

Having character flaws is very human. Doing nothing about them is tragic. Changing them is evidence that you are more than mere flesh and blood. Man reveals his spiritual nature through his transformation in character. The greatest evidence of the spirit working within man is the fact that character can change. You possess the ability to change. In fact you *are* the possibility of change, capable of a profoundly peaceful life if you choose it. You must be willing to let go of the character flaws that have been limiting you. It is simpler than you can imagine.

Are You Possessed by a Flaw?

Most of you know how incredibly difficult some people can be. "He's a bear to live with," or "What a character." These are expressions we have all used. You may not have a name for the particular character flaw, but you know what it looks like. It makes for great gossip and keeps our attention riveted. Archie Bunker had one—he was addicted to being right. Donald Duck had one—raging indignation. Popeye's Olive Oyl, had one—she was the perpetual victim to Brutus, who was both arrogant and intolerant.

Character flaws affect relationships. The know-it-all Ralph Kramden and his intolerant wife, Alice, built a marriage around their foibles. Flaws add flavor and zest to life while creating turmoil, chaos, and pain. For those of us who love excitement and romance, flaws also add intensity. They are often part of the key to making deep relationships work. When you overcome a defect in character or learn to tolerate those found in your partner you add a profound bond to long-term love.

So Why Change?

There are many reasons to work on character flaws, even if your life seems to be manageable. First of all, it is always good to strive for perfection. Changing what you can is the courageous thing to do, and life needs to be lived courageously. Second, character flaws tend to spin around in your emotional world like a hurricane ready to hit the coast. They have power to disrupt your relationships. A flaw can suddenly become much more severe. Worse yet, one character defect can trigger others to surface. Third, flaws are automatic—they occur without your permission. When you are possessed by a flaw it chooses when to surface and you are a hostage. Fourth, the worse they get the more you will deny that you have flaws. That is a problem in and of itself.

Character flaws tend to come in clusters. Intolerance can trigger anger, which can kick in a feeling of rejection or inadequacy. These clusters can spin and perpetuate themselves. You only need to get one flaw going and the others automatically join. When they are all working in combination you are out of control. When they are out of *your* control, your life becomes unmanageable. I guarantee that when they are out of control, you have made the lives of others unmanageable too. This is what I mean when I say that your are possessed by the character flaw. If it possesses you, then you are past due for an emotional tune-up. Humans can't go a hundred thousand miles without a tune-up. We need to constantly correct our flaws. The good news is that correcting them has many rewards.

Two Goals of This Book

Let me suggest two goals to you: your first goal should be to transform your own character; your second should be to learn how to survive the flaws of others. When you achieve these two goals, you will automatically become more successful in relationships and in business. You will be a better parent, a better friend, and a wonderful spouse.

Now I know that every self-help book you have ever read tells you that you must change your beliefs in order to change yourself. They never seem to be specific about what it takes to change a belief. I will be very specific. I don't want to leave you with an excuse not to change.

After you adopt new beliefs we will talk about mastering the use of wholesome qualities, much the same way you would use a character flaw. It is a little more difficult at first. Being honest doesn't come easily or automatically if you have been dishonest for a long time. Peacefulness is torture for the rage addict. I'll show you how to gently change.

You cannot, however, change the beliefs of others. You can suggest alternative beliefs or demonstrate that you believe differently. You can't push a rope.

As my friend Charlie "Tremendous" Jones would say, "You can lead a horse to water, but you can't make him drink. You *can* put salt in his oats." The most important thing to surviving the character flaws of others is to find the good intention or the need behind the flaw. When you discover the hidden need it is as though you just salted those oats. You see, you will have discovered the hole in a person's soul.

Holes in Your Soul

I'll bet you can spot a person with holes in his or her soul. Have you ever complimented someone on how she looks, only to have her deny it and point out her flaws? Have you ever called someone on his bad behavior only to have him point out why *you* are the problem? Or maybe you know a teenager? They all have holes in their soul, unfulfilled needs that drive them to adopt character defects in order to survive. Teenagers are changing so rapidly that they don't have time to hide their "stuff" the way adults do. But you can spot it easily enough. Look at the individual who wants everybody to like him. He lies, distorts, and makes up things as he goes along, just to fit in or be appreciated. Unless you are living in a cave someplace you see them all the time.

Most of your flawed associates don't want to change. When they do decide that it is time to change they start working on their personality, which is more superficial than character, and easier to affect. That's like treating a skin disease with makeup. Most of my colleagues will tell you that it takes years of hard work in therapy to make profound changes in the personality. Many of them will also tell you that you are stuck with your character. You can't change it.

Don't you believe that for a moment. In my twenty years as a psychiatrist, I have seen some of the most miraculous transformations in character in my patients. The good news is that the character change seems to be simpler, sometimes almost effortless. Not that you can change without effort. It is just that some people have such a profound transformation that it can only be explained by the word "miracle."

What is the key to this miraculous character change we see in some seriously flawed individuals? Do these severely flawed beings hold the secret to a pattern that we can adopt? My take on it is that the key to this profound transformation is a willingness to change, a kind of humility. You don't have to be strong willed, just willing. In fact it seems that the weaker one is, while humbly admitting the need to change, the more profound the change. Grace falls like rain on the good and the bad. The hungrier the crop the more it can absorb.

Willingness to change is not the same as changing by self will. Willingness is the humility to expose a hole in your soul. It is the honesty to admit that there is a need that hasn't been filled with all your attempts, efforts, and exertions. There is an empty feeling that can't be relieved by obsession, confession, or possession. You can use a flaw for control, power, or manipulation, but in the end you are no better off because a basic need still lies unfulfilled.

This is an unusual self-help book because I am not asking you to be strong to improve yourself. I am not asking you to be motivated and to go into action, to be passionate and energetic, but to weaken a bit, to soften up, to be less rigid. I am not promising you more intelligence and pizzazz but more wisdom, humility, and character.

Sanity, responsibility, and serenity are the goals of this transformation. It isn't talent that will take you there, but willingness. If you are distressed enough to be willing to change, something is going to happen. There is a core of goodness in every individual that has been programmed to help you grow. Some people have their emotional growth stunted at an early age because of abuse, trauma, alcohol, or drugs. Still the process of transforming aches to occur. The patient's soul is longing to grow up, trapped in a body of an individual whose emotional growth is stunted. Eventually, with a little help, the journey starts.

Are You Bored, Lonely, Inadequate, or Feeling Trapped?

You might notice that some really high achievers are running on empty, emotionally. They are trying to fill a hole that causes them to feel inadequate, unappreciated, or disapproved of by others.

In fact all these needs and negative feelings are unconsciously connected to what we believe about ourselves at the core of our being. Today there are many people whose beliefs are so out of whack that they are having an emotional-core meltdown. It is a spiritual problem in essence that shows up as a character crisis. I get excited when I see someone in crisis. I know that there is a power within you that will find the right stuff to fill the hole in your soul. The crisis is a signal that it is time to find meaning within. It is a time to look at your stuff to create a life of peace, joy, and self-esteem.

You can only go backwards so far before you run into something that causes you to change direction. I learned this vividly when I did my residency training while living in New York. We used to park our cars using a technique learned at the bumper-car ride in amusement parks. Back up till it goes bang, then pull forward. It doesn't work well in other parts of the country, but in NYC it is quite effective.

We do the same thing with our emotions. We back away from taking a good look at the beliefs we live by until we can go no further. When you can no longer live with what you believe, it is time to start changing beliefs. Changing beliefs will influence your character.

Character flaws hold the secret to wholeness. They hold the key to knowing how to fill in the holes in your soul.

What usually happens, though, is we try to fill the holes in our soul with ego. We develop swollen, inflated, or puffy egos.

Puffy Ego Syndrome

Okay, you can't find the term in any psychiatric literature. That's because I made it up. It simply means an ego that tries to compensate for low self-esteem by making itself larger.

Your ego puffs itself up and tries to plug the holes with defective exaggerations of character, and your flaws get worse. Your ego is trying to help you survive. It helped you learn social graces and keep you toilet trained. It has done a pretty good job. In fact your ego has learned how to be creative in using character flaws. In my years of treating patients I have found ten flaws that occur most frequently.

THE TEN MOST COMMON CHARACTER FLAWS

1. Addicted to being right
2. Raging indignation
3. Fixing blame and nurturing resentments
4. The dread seekers—worry and fear
5. Intolerance
6. The poor me or martyr syndrome
7. Self-regard run riot
8. The excuse for everything—inadequacy
9. Hypercritical fault finders
10. Chronic dishonesty—the trap

Sparkle Like a Gem

This book is designed to help you shed some of these ten flaws. It may also help you put some new defenses to work with people who have always gotten to you before. When you finish this book, expect that your character will sparkle like a finely cut gem, but don't expect to be finished. If you are still alive when the last page is read, that is a sign that you still have some change to go through and more fun to experience.

This is a book about hope. You already have everything you need to get going. If you have identified one of the character flaws as your own, don't focus too hard on it. Start exploring the wholesome quality that could replace it and make your life better.

You also do not have to read the chapters in order. You know what you need better than I do. If you want to skip to the chapter that seems appropriate, then go to it. You don't even have to finish this first chapter. Follow your own sequence. Or ask a friend which one you need to read first. Make sure it's an honest friend, though, someone who will tell you the truth.

Did You Laugh at Yourself Today?

A real sign of maturity is the ability to laugh at yourself. I hope you take yourself a little less seriously after you read this book. Re-creating yourself, changing your destiny, is serious, but criticism from others really isn't. When you start to change I guarantee that some well-meaning friend or relative will try to get you to be your old self. They will get a bit uncomfortable with the changes they see. They were used to your goofy behavior and would like to see it continue. If they are offering you criticism out of love and not the need to be right, then accept it if it is true and be amused if it isn't.

Remember that the goal of transformation is profound peace and loving relationships. You don't need all this aggravation just to fulfill the need to be right or to be admired.

Life is a gift to you. Your life can be a blessing to others. Your character is the wrapping that the gifts of your soul are packaged in. Make it a work of art. The world will be a better place if you do.

Addicted to Being Right

HOW DO YOU KNOW IF YOU ARE *ADDICTED TO BEING RIGHT?*

1. Would you rather be right than happy?
2. Is Archie Bunker your role model for personal relationships?
3. Is being right the foundation for relationships?
4. Is being right worth dying for?
5. Are you unsettled until someone else agrees with you?
6. Do you enjoy arguing even when you know it is creating ill will?
7. Do you have to have the last word in an argument?
8. Do you find yourself discussing disagreements long after they are finished, just to prove you were right?
9. Do you believe that because you have a feeling that you are right, you must be right?

10. Do you continuously bother to argue facts with people who are concerned only with feelings?

11. Does proving your point of view take precedent over listening to others?

12. Does being right feel normal?

13. Even after being demonstrated wrong, do you still search for ways to prove your point of view?

14. Is your opinion more important than fact?

15. Let's face it, are you nearly always right except when you think you might be wrong?

16. Does being right feel crucial?

17. Does being right feel like a solution?

18. Do you thrive on crisis?

19. If you admitted you were wrong, would it shock your partner?

"What's the most common addiction, Doc?" asked the interviewer, who thought he knew more about substance abuse than I did, because he'd had a bout with cocaine addiction. "The most common," I said, pausing while the camera zoomed in, "is the addiction to being right. When the need to be right is so strong that a person will sell his soul to satisfy this craving, you have a person with a deadly addiction."

The entire crew started to laugh. Even the interviewer realized he was more interested in being right than in hearing my opinion.

I'd Rather Be Right Than Happy!

Every time someone comes to me complaining that they are right, and unhappy that others don't agree, I ask them if they would rather be right or happy. That is one of the most important questions you can ask yourself. It's not as though you can't be both, but how often do we spin our wheels uselessly trying to get someone to agree with us? We want to be told we are right even if we have to be miserable to get there.

Addicted to being right isn't just having a strong opinion and sticking by it. Churchill had strong opinions and stuck by them. The world is a better place now because of him. No, it is that unending need to have people agree with you or else you don't feel settled. I had a friend in medical school who used to love to debate. He would argue about any point simply to show he could win the argument. I was never sure he believed even half of what he was saying, but he loved to win arguments.

Even though it isn't politically correct to say so, I have noticed men and women use this character defect differently. Men tend to use their addiction to being right to control, force an agreement, and make others give in. Women tend to use it to get others to agree that they have been mistreated or forced to do something against their will. Men are more aggressive, women more passive. If you don't like that, don't blame me, blame God. He's responsible.

Shock Your Partner, Admit You're Wrong!

When couples fight, they often leave the issue that started the fight and argue about who's right. One of these days, right in the middle of a fight, admit you are wrong. Watch what happens. Usually your partner is taken by surprise. Half the time he or she couldn't care less and wants to continue to fight. If that's the case he or she will quickly find something else that you're wrong about.

There is hope, though. For those of you who think it is really much too difficult to admit not being right, watch a couple who have been together for a long time and are happy. Someone quickly admits to being wrong. When you admit you're wrong, something very strange happens. Your partner will start to question whether or not he or she is actually right.

In a relationship or friendship the addiction to being right usually stems from one party playing the teacher/educator and the other playing the student. One is wiser and the other needy. This need to be a teacher or the wiser one is an issue of control and power. The teacher is the one in charge, whose will is to be obeyed.

My friend Joe is only mildly afflicted. He doesn't claim to be always right, but his ideas are always a little better than yours. So when you disagree with his good ideas, he keeps coming at you to try and convince you that his way is better. Even when it doesn't really matter he wants his way to be recognized as better. He isn't argumentative, but he can't really be happy with two coexisting points of view. You must admit his is better.

> **A man must be both stupid and uncharitable who believes there is no virtue or truth but on his own side.**
> **—JOSEPH ADDISON**

My father was a much more severe case of ATBR. Dad used to say that the only time he was wrong was when he thought he was wrong. Otherwise he was always right. He wouldn't dare make the mistake of thinking he was wrong about something. Being wrong once was more than enough for him. We all have our methods of coping with people like that. I became a psychiatrist.

To a certain extent, everyone has the belief that his way of living and doings things is right. That is why it is a cultural shock to see people living peaceful, joyful lives without doing it our way. Culture shock is cured by open-mindedness. Living overseas is a great way to develop an open-minded attitude.

You're So Smart You're Starting to Sound Stupid!

I had an aunt who had a great deal of common sense. She didn't have a lot of education by today's standards, but she was still quite smart and could see through people. I once saw her look a man in the eye and tell him, "You're so smart, you're starting to sound stupid to me." That's a great approach to dealing with a person you never have to see again. People who need to be right think the world needs them for their great wisdom. Often they are misguided.

Think about how many times you have had to listen to someone's current theory of how to solve the world's problems. It is all theory, never tested. Most people want to test it on you, with your money and in your community.

> **Those who never retract their opinions love themselves more than they love truth.**
> **—JOSEPH JOUBER**

People addicted to being right don't always sound stupid. They are often very eloquent. But they are usually stuck. That's a key. Being stuck is a defining symptom of being addicted to being right. The easiest way to identify a person who is ATBR is to see how badly he is stuck. Watch an argument and notice if the "right" person can muster even a little understanding of your point of view. If the person's focus is entirely on making sure you understand why he is right, the person is stuck. These people believe that if you don't agree with them, then they haven't explained themselves clearly enough, so they keep coming at you, over and over again. They also confuse listening to your point of view with waiting to talk.

You know what happens. A couple starts an argument. One, usually the woman, wants to discuss feelings. The other, usually the man, wants to discuss facts. She knows intuitively that the facts don't matter. Worse yet she realizes that he doesn't have the same feelings about the issue that she does. He knows logically that her feelings are out of whack. To him they don't fit what his picture of the situation is. They start to talk, to verbalize, to communicate, to confess, to declare, divulge, unmask. . . . That's right—they decide to drive each other crazy. Each is addicted to being right. She thinks that because she feels it, it is right. He is certain that logically, he is right. She believes her intuitive flashes are some sort of profound knowledge. He can logically prove his point, therefore it must be truth.

Too bad her feelings are often based on issues from her past and he's missed the point, using logic to defend himself. They go around and around on their emotional carousel and slowly it becomes part of the roller coaster of their life. Both of them would like to stop but can't because they are right. After all, you have to stand for principle. The road to divorce is paved with such principles.

In therapy with this type of couple we would give them a way out, an exit ramp that they could take as the roller coaster came to the top of a steep drop. "Admit that you may not be right, but that the issue was important to you. Tell your partner that you respect his/her right to see it differently." Patients always understand that they can cancel the argument and choose peace, but they rarely do. The excuse is, "This time I knew I was right." And of course if I could prove I was right, then I could be happy.

I'm Right but I'm Such High Maintenance

Many of us stay addicted to being right because our self-esteem is linked to proving that what we believe is true. If I am right I am worthwhile, and if I am wrong I am inadequate. Addicted to being right is associated with untested beliefs and good intentions. "If I have good intentions I am worthwhile" gradually changes to "If I have good intentions I must be right!" The flaw is associated with a lack of open-mindedness and willingness to listen to the beliefs of others. All the self-help books in the world can't do a thing for you without some open-mindedness. You can't operate in the realm of ideas, because contrary ideas aggravate you.

Let's talk about the issue of self-esteem. I define self-esteem as that feeling of value you place on yourself based on your view of your past history, your body, and your thoughts. Ultimately, at some deep level it has to do with who you believe you are in the depths of your being. People with high self-esteem are rarely addicted to being right, whereas low self-esteem makes people less resourceful and more prone to being addicted to being right. These folks are less resourceful because they don't believe they have the right to develop new capabilities. They don't deserve them.

The problem is that self-esteem doesn't teach well because self-esteem isn't a skill. Self-esteem is the by-product of feeling good about yourself. I believe it is far better to teach resourcefulness and resiliency and give people the opportunity to enhance their ability to be productive. Then self-esteem will take care of itself.

I have a friend who works for a very bright boss in the automotive industry. His boss loves to have everything done his way. The hardest thing at work is to get enough evidence to change the man's mind. It can be pure torture. After all, you have to deal with the person's inadequacy before you can get to the facts or issues. The whole time the boss may be going around in circles trying to avoid looking at what is important. He is wedded to his position because his self-esteem is invested in being right. Round and round you go, hoping somehow to get somewhere.

Being right all the time is high maintenance. Being right requires facts and careful justification. It also demands an ability to distort facts, to make excuses, and to blame others. Being right all the time means dealing with all these people who are wrong except when they agree with you—and that can be tiring as well as frustrating.

> **To be positive: to be mistaken at the top of one's voice.**
> **—AMBROSE BIERCE**

The addictive solution is to surround yourself with people who see it your way. That solves the problem of arguing temporarily, but it makes the flaw a lot worse by reinforcing it. The person addicted to being right deludes himself into believing he is always right. He'd rather be right than happy anyway. He believes being right will control his happiness and self-esteem.

The need to be right is based upon an overriding desire to be in control. Don't resist me on this one, I am right and I can justify it. I'm writing this book and I'm in control of the ideas here! I'm positive, convinced! Silly, isn't it? People who are caught by this flaw always sound so adolescent. Their need for external control is matched by their internal disorder. It is the by-product of low self-esteem.

Duty or responsibility is at issue too. Most people want responsibility but don't want to follow the path of duty or right behavior. They want responsibility only if they can be in control or receive praise. The actions that they take are always justified in their own minds, even if they are immoral. Duty isn't the issue for them—needs and convenience are. Their own needs create the justification they use for immoral behavior.

The person who is stuck in the flaw can't ever admit being wrong, because being wrong is a blow to the ego. Being wrong is equated with danger or shame. This is a character flaw that works with the heart through denial and with the intellect through rationalization. It specializes in people who like relationships in which they get to play parent or teacher—authority figures who can exert control. You can't marry a guidance counselor or therapist. It doesn't work.

Take for instance a married couple I saw who fought viciously for years. Each was addicted to being right. They came to see me claiming they wanted desperately to stay together. When they arrived for a session they described the pattern of how they fought. What they did was relatively common. The couple argued and it escalated. When it got loud enough and crazy enough she then charged he was victimizing her. At that point he stormed out angrily. They came to me because something had precipitated an urgent call for help. No, they hadn't been physically violent. Recently the children had stopped taking sides and told their parents to grow up.

A grammar school principal and his wife came in with a similar scenario. The wife had said something the husband felt the need to correct. He was, after all, the man of wisdom that she had sought all her life to rescue her from her crazy family. The reactions were fast and furious. She disagreed. The husband, who was always right, felt inadequate and threatened. He required her to listen to and accept his wonderful advice. The wife felt she was being treated like a child and got angry. It was never safe for her to display anger around him, so she played the victim. The message to him was that if he were a good husband he wouldn't victimize her. He walked out.

Being Right Feels Like a Solution!

"I may not be able to fix the problem, but at least I'm right about what's wrong!" If I had a million dollars for every time someone said that and realized it was idiotic I'd be destitute. We all believe that knowing what is wrong is half the solution. We stress diagnosis in medicine. There are specialists in every field who analyze the problem and recommend solutions. The problem with people who are addicted to being right is they are lulled into believing their own diagnosis. In medicine we say that if you are being diagnosed by yourself, your doctor is a fool.

Insisting you're right about something may be the best you can do in the situation, but it doesn't mean you're right. All it means is you've responded to the problem with your opinion. Most of the time we identify what we think is wrong. More than half the time we identity other people as the cause of our problems. We try to keep power, control, and respect as well as look righteous in the eyes of others while blaming them for what is wrong. In case you haven't figured it out, that doesn't work. That's one of the reasons why it is so important to identify this character flaw.

A patient come to my office and said, "Dr. T. I have been in therapy for seventeen years and I'm still miserable." My response was to ask how she managed to find different therapists for nearly two decades who would agree with her. The last thing a person addicted to being right needs is a therapist who sits there and agrees with him or her.

How Is ATBR Useful?

Flaws don't occur because people are bad but because people are hurting, insecure, or beaten up by life. Character flaws are a response to a problem, not a solution. When you are dealing with someone who is addicted to being right, it is a signal to tread easily. For friends it signals an opportunity to practice tolerance. The person isn't nearly as tough as he or she pretends to be. It is a call to kindness, clothed in arrogant robes. It is a scared child grown up afraid that if what he or she believes isn't true, life will become a bigger mess. When I start arguing with my wife, Barbara, and insisting I'm right, she calls a time-out. She'll say, "Can we take a break for a moment. I just wanted to stop and tell you I love you very much." That blows the steam out of my boiler pretty fast.

Duty and Dignity

No matter where you go on the face of the earth, you will find that society is based on a moral presupposition. It is that we must strive to do the right thing for ourselves, our family, and our community. The idea of duty is the common denominator behind human dignity. For someone who has been abused as a child, however, this high-minded idealism goes astray. On some level the rules start to change because the environment is fraught with danger. A young child who grows up with rules that are hard to understand and that constantly change gets frantic trying to figure out what is right. Truth no longer is the issue behind duty, but survival is. We slowly become focused on our rights and not our responsibilities.

This represents a big challenge. If being wrong was dangerous, being right becomes critical. Doing the right thing one day is the wrong thing the next. A child needs to know that doing the right thing will be rewarded with safety, security, and love. Instead we have millions of children growing up with selfish parents who change the rules to fit their convenience. It is terrifying. In the child's mind, the solution is to make sure he is right. So the child spends a lot of time and effort making sure. Little by little being right becomes a solution. It is reassuring. The child gets addicted to being right, or worse yet plays the game of always being wrong, so that he or she can control the other person's being right. You know the type. It is usually a woman in a relationship with an arrogant man who must be right. Her safety depends on making sure she agrees. It's emotional suicide. Either way insistence on being right feels safer than risking being wrong.

The real goal is stability. Addicts are always running after something. At first it is the high. Later it is just the attempt to feel normal.

Being Right Feels Like Being Stable

Just like the drug addict using heroin, being right is the solution. It is soothing, relieves pain, and takes care of one's cravings for approval and appreciation. It adds steadiness to a life that is missing stability. It reverses the self-esteem withdrawal syndrome that the person who needs to be right goes through whenever he is wrong.

To add stability to your life all you really have to do is to make sure that what you believe is true. You don't have to convince other people of it. Even people who believe that disaster always happens will feel stable in a crisis.

An ER nurse, addicted to excitement and crisis, came to my office complaining that her relationships with men had all been a disaster. "All men are pigs," she said. "They all are the same. They want one thing. They abuse you and make your life miserable. They are emotional midgets who should be castrated."

> People do not seem to realize that their opinion of the world is also a confession of character.
> —RALPH WALDO EMERSON

I had a hunch that she was angry.

You should have seen the men she chose to date. They were a mixture of alcoholics, drug addicts, and gamblers who all cheated on her. She was able to do a great job in the ER because it represented security. Every day she could go into the hospital and have the assurance that life was consistently chaotic and ferociously stable. Violence, trauma, and tragedy were reassuring. She couldn't see how her beliefs about men were coming true through the relationships she had. She could, however, sense how reassured she felt in the ER. The turmoil in the ER helped her feel stable. The turmoil she experienced with men did the same. She just hated admitting it because she would have to admit that some of her beliefs about men were wrong.

A human being will do just about anything to defend a belief that is taking care of a deep need. Religious fanatics will kill or commit suicide en masse for their beliefs. Children will get depressed over losing a belief in Santa. A woman will date some of the creepiest guys in order to prove that men are real creeps.

Addicted to being right comes about in order to help you survive. Sometimes a belief that was useful, even lifesaving, gets firmly entrenched. When you believe that it will protect you from annihilation, then of course you get addicted to it.

If you are having trouble understanding how chaos could feel normal, remember that people who need to be right often grew up with chaos. Getting back to your childhood roots feels great. My experience with hundreds of patients with this flaw leads me to conclude that being right develops in children who grow up in families where being wrong was dangerous. These are the children of hypercritical and emotionally and physically abusive parents. These are the children whose safety seemed to be assured by being right just like their parents. These are the children who grew up with parents who had addictive beliefs, beliefs that caused pain and suffering but that they were unwilling to give up. They grow up needing chaos to feel normal and adopt many of their parents' addictive beliefs.

If Being Wrong Was Dangerous—Being Right Is Crucial!

After years of listening to stories that would make your hair stand on end I often wonder how some people turn out so well. We humans are a terribly resourceful folk. So often children grow up in environments

The foolish and the dead alone never change their opinions.
—JAMES RUSSELL LOWELL

that aren't emotionally or physically safe. Yet they not only cope but often turn it into some sort of talent.

Addicted to being right is a terrific coping mechanism that has gone awry. You have heard the expressions "Stick by your guns no matter what," "You've gotta do the right thing," or "A man's gotta do what a man's gotta do."

Preaching and Sleeping with the Choir

> **Convictions are more dangerous foes of truth than lies.**
> —FRIEDRICH NIETZSCHE

A while back I entered the office of a minister friend of mine. He gave wonderful sermons, dressed in the finest clothing, drove the finest cars, and looked stunning on TV, speaking about spiritual transformation. The problem was that he had numerous affairs with women who were members of his church. A number of them had called me to discuss what to do.

The episode was a disaster. He sincerely believed having an affair with a man as great as him was beneficial to the ladies. He also sincerely wanted to help everyone be perfect like he was. He had strong convictions that his behavior was just.

> **To be absolutely certain about something, one must know everything or nothing about it.**
> —OLIN MILLER

Underlying his grandiosity was a deep-seated inadequacy. I never even got near the issues before he threw me out of the office. I wanted to turn to him as I was leaving and say, "Hey, Reverend, show me your morals." It would have been useless. He was ATBR, eloquent, and doing it for the benefit of others. No matter how many people he had helped it was like a germ in a quart of milk. Even a little spoils the whole container.

We show our principles by practicing them rather than preaching them. We all know the best way to teach kids is to show them by our behavior. Little children who are told one thing and then see another tend to become addicted to being right. It's the perfect scenario; conflicting beliefs and turmoil. Remember, the chaos and the need to survive it creates the addiction. Conflicting beliefs are great for generating emotional chaos.

What Makes You the Authority?

People who are ATBR love to present themselves as authorities. Yet in most fields the great authorities are those who have been open-minded and paid attention to truth. ATBRs typically give you their closed-minded opinion. They are struggling to fit the world to their picture, their needs, so that they can feel okay.

Did You Learn Anything from Being Right?

Hopefully you now understand that being right may not be a solution to some problems. Actually, when it's an addiction it is its own problem. That's the bad news. The good news is that the addiction is fairly simple to let go of, as long as you can maintain some open-mindedness. For those of you who are terribly addicted to being right, remember that with a little open-mindedness you might learn something. Then you will have more you can be right about. You can start by getting yourself to see what you look like in reaction.

It is like disassociating from your body. Sound too strange? It is like looking at what you are doing from a place next to yourself. Most of the time we characterize a person who is severely stuck as being beside himself. When I realized that, I started asking patients to view their arguments from the side. It actually works.

Next time you are "stuck big-time" imagine that you are a detached observer watching the insanity from the side. The new point of view will help you see what the person looks like when "stuck." Chances are you use similar tones and expressions each time. You are on automatic pilot. That's a clue. Here's another; every time you are stuck, you sound like the voice of a parent or figure of authority from the past.

That should cause you to laugh a bit at yourself. Please, don't laugh out loud. You will trigger some very unwelcome reactions from your partner. By the way, when you are in an argument with someone and you are stuck—the other person is probably stuck too. We tend to find people to match us.

Being amused at yourself is another really useful tool. It helps to defuse the bomb. Most of us take ourselves too seriously. As Les Brown, the great motivational speaker, says, "Don't worry about the small stuff, and remember, it's all small stuff."

You might not even be arguing about anything true. Ask yourself that all-important question: "Suppose this isn't true from the other person's point of view?" Then there might not be any way to prove your point, because it just isn't so. The argument could become endless, like a born-again Christian arguing with a fundamentalist Muslim about God.

Since the final outcome of all good arguments is some sort of resolution, the next step is really quite logical. At some time or another you will wind up forgiving the person you are in the argument with. That is if you plan to continue a relationship with the person. Let's be realistic, you will eventually have to get over any resentment.

Why not do it first? Why not forgive, let go of resentment as a first step in resolving the difference? You're going to have to do it later anyhow. Why waste the time?

An alcoholic carpenter in recovery taught me to appreciate this one. "When I feel that I am arguing because I am addicted to being right, I just admit I'm wrong. I do that in the beginning for whatever I know I'm wrong about, Doc. There is always something, at least I can admit to being addicted to being right. Then I deal with the resentment right up front. It's faster to deal with the resentment first. I can see where I was wrong much quicker. The fights are shorter. It's like using the right end of the hammer to drive a nail."

If you do find yourself stuck in the midst of the flaw, go ahead and admit to what you happen to be wrong about. Just your side, your error, your unfounded belief. If you are stuck, then there is something, some fear related to a belief.

Work on your own beliefs, not others'. It's not your duty to then help the other person see where he or she is wrong. It really is easier being forgiving and wrong than it is to be right and resentful. If you realize that you have nothing that you are wrong about, please reread this chapter.

It really is simple. When you are stuck, this is all you have to do:

- Notice that you are in reaction
- Step aside and see what you look like
- Be amused with your ego
- Forgive yourself for being in reaction
- Silently forgive the other person
- Admit where you are wrong
- Work on your own beliefs

Whenever you get stuck, review and reset boundaries. An emotional boundary is a belief that you raise like a wall to define your personal territory. Everybody has them. If you are stuck, you stepped over one, or you brought someone into one of yours. Be clear about it. Let other people know when they are out of line. Let them know that they have crossed into areas that have too much pain attached. Boundaries change all the time. As we develop deeper relationships, they can be relaxed. But unless you are an ascended master, you will have some boundaries to take care of.

What happens when two people, both certain that they are right, get stuck? They develop an endless argument. It's like the song that never ends. It goes on and on because it's the argument that never ends. I believe it represents a return to the chaos that helped create a familiar misery. Step out of yourself and ask for a time-out. I often ask couples to give each other permission to call for a time-out. They reschedule the unending argument for somewhere and sometime else. Most of the time in the midst of an argument over something that you are sure you are right about, you won't give permission to take a break. You are propelled by the belief that if you win this one you will feel better.

Take a break and reschedule. Then watch as a detached observer and notice the resentments that need to be released. Identify what you believe gives you the right to argue addictively and you will find some need that you are trying to protect.

Remember to stick by what is duty and not to control, or worse yet, what is convenient for you. The reasons we are addicted to being right are usually wrong. It is useless to control others. We can't build our self-esteem on the ashes of another person's beliefs. Sometimes it is better to let old issues die rather than argue about them. Since there can be so many reasons for a person to be stuck, we need to have a higher reason for doing what we do. We need to make our relationship decisions based on what our duties and our responsibilities are. We can't make our decisions based on whether the other person is wrong about what he or she believes.

You know what your duties are in your various relationships, whether at home or at work. Do the right thing rather than stay addicted to knowing what is right.

Often arguments start as a cover for issues that are much bigger than people realize. They are not at all related to current situations. In the long run beating each other up to prove who is right won't make you happy. Somehow, somewhere, there was something that caused a deep need to be right. A person isn't bad because of it. He or she probably isn't going to change overnight, but you can always change yourself today.

What Is the Payoff?

I know you're not going to let go of this character flaw unless it benefits you. It will. Every time you become willing to let go of a flaw, your character changes for the better. Unseen talents will develop and you will become more whole. In fact my experience with hundreds of patients leads me to believe that your needs will be fulfilled better in some unforeseen way, if you let go of a flaw.

As I have stated, all of the character flaws discussed in this book will lead you to issues that you can grow through. A person addicted to being right has a great opportunity to practice tolerance and understanding. Remember that highest authority preaches acceptance, tolerance, and understanding. If this character flaw is going to give you the inside track on learning these profound principles, then it is a great blessing in disguise.

It's okay to be wrong. We all are sometimes. Though some of us are wrong a lot less than others. But who's keeping score? Only a person who needs to be right would do that. It may be okay to be wrong, but it is a sign of great self-esteem to humbly admit it. You will learn from it too. If you don't learn from being wrong, you're foolish.

Here are the lessons you will learn. You will learn what you actually believe, life criteria. You will learn that even if you are wrong you can be forgiven. You will learn that dealing with others who are addicted to being right can be fun, if you become a better listener. You will learn great tolerance in the process.

Dealing with people who are stuck is a great way to recognize that nourishment for your soul doesn't always come pleasantly wrapped. It usually comes cloaked with the flaws of others. Our spiritual gifts are shrouded in a cloak of intolerance, impatience, and fear.

Recognize this flaw and remember that the other person is seeking love and approval. Dealing with an argumentative, self-righteous person is a gift that allows you to give even when the other person is obviously wrong. The belief that your spouse, friend, or boss is stuck on must have value on some level. That means you are being given the opportunity to validate someone and to look at both sides of the issue as you do it. The hidden mysteries of the soul often are covered with the veneer of desperately needing to be right. The belief that we addictively hold is often a casing in which old pain, old trauma lies buried. Be respectful.

When you are freed from this flaw, you will immediately see a change in your energy. The passion and power that you invested in believing something so strongly that it was like a drug to you will be released. Your life will be filled with renewed purpose.

It's Okay to Be Miserable As Long As You Are Happy About It!

The suffering in life is not optional, but the misery is. If you choose misery be happy about it. I am not saying you shouldn't hold on to a belief that is important. Please do, but be joyful about it. You can't avoid some misery being associated with holding firmly to your beliefs. As long as they are not addictions, it's okay.

Charles "Tremendous" Jones, the great motivational speaker, has a signature vignette. He talks about being happy that he has so much misery. That's a key to moving away from this character flaw.

It really is okay to be miserable, as long as you are happy about it. The problem with most people is that when they are in misery, they really are miserable about it. In fact the miserable of the world progress to the next character flaw, raging indignation.

Raging Indignation

HOW DO YOU KNOW IF YOU HAVE *RAGING INDIGNATION?*

1. Do you get angry even when it would be wiser to stay in control?
2. Does arguing feel more normal than discussion?
3. Do you use your rage to control or intimidate others?
4. Do you sometimes stop and wonder, "How did I get so upset?"
5. Are others put off or frightened by your anger?
6. Does anger feel like a rush, almost thrilling?
7. Do you think a good argument is a lot of fun?
8. Do you get outraged in public and embarrass your friends and family?
9. Do you argue with strangers?

10. Do you berate employees or even your boss from time to time?

11. Do people frequently ask you to calm down?

12. Do you use the excuse that "I'm Irish, or Italian, or German" or some other ethnicity for being upset?

13. Is being upset your only emotion?

14. Do people say, "He's a nice guy but don't get him upset," about you?

15. Do you feel better about yourself when you are enraged?

16. Are you known for your short fuse?

17. Do you like to stoke other people's rage?

18. Do you sometimes look for an excuse to be upset?

19. Do you make a villain out of certain people so you can vent your anger and be justified?

The first day I ever set foot in Italy I got a lesson in raging indignation that I will never forget. My dad and I were driving out of the Milan airport. Two cars were stopped at the light. The drivers were out of their cars, yelling at each other over the top of one of the little Fiats. If this had occurred in the Bronx, both of them would have pulled guns. I had never seen people argue this loudly in public except at a riot in Manhattan.

These two men were gesticulating violently, but neither of them pulled a gun or a knife. They just yelled and screamed. The light turned green, and with that typical Italian shrug of their shoulders, they smiled and got back into their cars. At the next light they repeated it. I couldn't resist and asked what they were fighting about. One of the men, on hearing my English turned and said, "Eh, *Americano,* we fight over *calcio*, soccer. Only women are more important."

Indignation is anger that is aroused by something we consider unjust or unworthy. Often it is an appropriate response, for instance when we learn of a small child who has been abused. Raging indignation is anger gone out of control. It is a character flaw that justifies flying into an angry rage to serve any purpose it chooses. When people can't get their way and get enraged or when people are caught doing something wrong, they rage on rather than admit their own guilt. It is a character flaw when you use rage rather than face your emotions. When the purpose of being indignant is to feed your ego at the expense of the well-being of others, you have this character flaw.

Righteous indignation is getting angry when it is your duty or obligation. It is when any normal person would be upset. You know righteous indignation when you see it; someone upset about life who decides to make changes. The righteously indignant make the world a better place. They are doing the right thing, and are willing to get emotional over it. We become indignant for the sake of showing that we care, like when we defend a loved one or find that someone has betrayed our trust. I have no issue with showing emotions. In fact the first time my wife really got upset and started yelling at me, I said to her, "You do care, don't you?" She thought I was crazy. She didn't grow up in an Italian-American household.

People are dangerously indignant when they are raging. These people are like raging bulls. Their discontent is raging indignation, not righteous indignation. The raging indignant, however, don't want to change anything but are looking for something to be indignant about. Anger creates a rush. Why is that?

Anger Is a Drug for Some People!

The two men at the airport in Milan were having fun, I suppose. They live in a culture that enjoys intense emotions. Here in the United States we would consider them out of place, yet there are millions of people who are just as indignant, angry, and incensed.

Turlough McConnell of the Celtic Vision once told me that the Irish aren't happy unless they are angry. But angry behavior doesn't always mean that the character flaw is surfacing. It takes a lot more passion to express yourself in Ireland or Italy than it does in England or Switzerland.

Anger becomes a character flaw when it is used like a drug for the rush. When you hear someone with this flaw he usually is worked up about nothing. It really amounts to raging bull. It is inflicted on others to feed one's own ego—the raging indignation makes the person feel revved up and alive. He or she is addicted to excitement. Sometimes it is a passive individual who is frustrated by not being able to manipulate someone.

From Simmer to Scorch

> He that is slow to wrath is of great understanding; but he that is hasty of spirit exalts folly.
> —PROVERBS 14:29

Sometimes the little fire we start gets totally out of control. We see it all the time—a gradual shift from simmering to scorch. People heating up are probably trying to signal to you that they don't feel good about life. It is their way of telling you they need space. Sometimes, though, you'll run into people who want to drop bombs on you and not expect anything in return. At least that is the way they act. They insult you and get really annoyed, irritable, or hostile. They hope that by showing you their irritability you will back off and leave them alone.

The usual scenario, though, is a slow intensification of emotions. We all have a boiling point or a flash point. With people who are consumed by the fires of raging indignation, the flash point comes much faster. The boiling point is lower. Tolerance is not nearly as great.

Let's look at what might be your fairly typical transition—going from annoyed to indignant. You get annoyed. Usually because something happened that you believe you shouldn't have to put up with.

The next emotion is frustration or irritability. Frustration means you want to persist to do it your way and you haven't given up. Irritability implies that it is starting to bother you more than you would like. Then you move to real anger. So far it's all very normal. Some people avoid the anger or turn it inward and feel disappointment. Finally, indignation, rage, and violence round out the

> **The greatest remedy for anger is delay.**
> **—SENECA**

flow of things. A normal person will experience three or four emotional transitions before he or she explodes (see chart 1 on page 36).

The raging indignant have a much more abrupt way of dealing with annoyance. They go right to violence. They cut to the chase and short-circuit everything. They also justify why it is okay to get so out of control. They then go ballistic (see chart 2 on page 37).

Donald Duck Meets Nikita Khrushchev

Speaking of ballistic, do you remember the Cuban Missile Crisis? We saw a great example of someone out of control. Chairman Khrushchev was shown on TV, pounding his shoe on the table at the General Assembly of the United Nations. I was a child at the time, and watched the Three Stooges and Donald Duck afterward. I couldn't help noticing the similarities in temperament. The problem was, however, the enraged Khrushchev had enough thermonuclear power to fry the entire United States. At least Donald and Mo were doing it for entertainment. They used raging indignation for comedy. It usually isn't funny when you are on the receiving end. In the movie *Raging Bull*, the lead character embodies the devastation this flaw inflicts. He loses control of his temper and beats anything that gets in his way. De Niro portrays a man who is possessed by his rage and can't control it. The rage has a life of its own.

Next time you see a cartoon with that wonderful duck in it, watch his reactions. It will help you identify the methods used by so many to go "ballistic" when they choose to. Raging indignation is

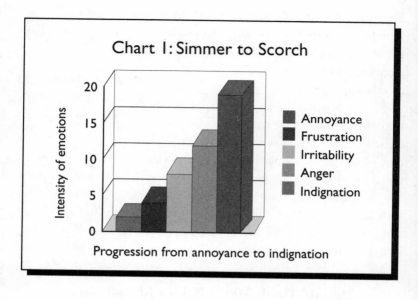

Chart 1: Simmer to Scorch

Intensity of emotions

20
15
10
5
0

Annoyance
Frustration
Irritability
Anger
Indignation

Progression from annoyance to indignation

a character flaw that has many variations. Isn't it interesting, though, that Nikita Khrushchev wanted most of all to go to Disneyland? Raging bulls aren't all bad. It's just that some people believe they are at their best when they are enraged, incensed, or indignant.

Sharks Don't Have Valium Receptors

Baby Paul, a young guy who used to play the game of pretending to be connected to the mob, came to my office one day after having car trouble. He said, "I need an emergency session, Dr. T. I'm having some difficulties dealing with my automobile."

He had the strangest sound in his voice when he said "automobile." He sounded like a man going into a trance.

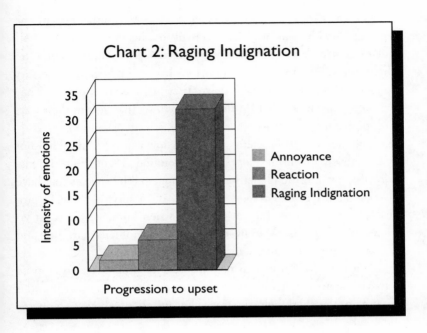

"I got pissed and beat up the new Z," Paul said. "The stereo wasn't working right, and I was getting really angry, so I took a time-out. I got out of the car and locked the key in the ignition. Then I smashed the side window to get in. When I cut my hand I went ballistic. I smashed all the windows and probably would have set the thing on fire if the troopers hadn't shown up. They arrested me on I-95. The judge told me I had to get psychiatric help. I told the judge I already had a shrink and he let me out."

> An angry man is again angry with himself when he returns to reason.
> —PUBLILIUS SYRUS

He was like a shark in a feeding frenzy. As soon as he saw the sight of blood he was off. Like a convulsion, his rage was completely out of control. Sharks, by the way, don't have Valium receptors in their brains. Valium receptors didn't evolve until it became necessary to be calm. Sharks can't calm down, they just feed on violence. They are eating machines that rip through anything that gets in their way. You probably know a few sharks in your private ocean too.

The capacity to be calm and settle down to relax and chill out is a relatively recent development in evolution. Throughout the history of the world the planet has been populated by species that have had the ability to be enraged, not calm. It's a survival thing. It protects most life-forms. It is at its worst when humans, the most vicious animals to have ever lived, get enraged. Humans start wars and are more destructive than any other species.

Anger naturally turns to rage in order to protect us, to help us survive when just being angry doesn't do the trick. Rage for the piranha or the shark helps it survive because that is how it competes for food.

Animals capable of great rage and lacking the ability to be calm generally have no respect for life. Doesn't it sound like a former employer or someone you went to school with? There is a similarity. The issue is respect for life. It requires peacefulness. The character flaw of raging indignation requires an enormous amount of selfishness and a lack of respect for the rights of others. Life is sacred. When you truly believe that it is sacred, rage becomes unethical and rarely useful. It is only ethical when it is used to help you survive great danger.

There have been studies showing that the fight-or-flight reaction, that ability for animals to react to danger with an automatic release of hormones and to survive, is activated many times faster than is the ability to chill out. Fight or flight is the physiological basis for this character flaw. With that you should conclude that fighting is necessary for survival, and useful sometimes. It's a little different when it becomes a character flaw that possesses you. Then it is no longer related to real danger. Your flaw put the "d" in front of anger and creates the danger.

It Doesn't Take Anyone to Get You Mad

If you already planned on being upset, then it doesn't matter who gets in your way. The raging indignant plan to be upset, actually long for it. It makes them feel alive, whole, and powerful. Often they seek out the weak because they know it is safer to go ballistic on someone who is defenseless. Others are just convenient targets for the abuse. Being a target of someone else's rage is not pleasant. Worse yet, the raging indignant try to convince you it was not premeditated.

Upset!

A patient with a chronic history of violence came into my office to tell me that he was "upset" when he beat his girlfriend. He used the word "upset" to describe how he felt when he beat people, fought with strangers, argued with police over moving violations. "Upset" was an umbrella emotion, his way of feeling safe, empowered, and forcing people to accept him. He didn't need anyone in particular to be upset with. It was as natural for him as breathing. Too bad he couldn't stand the reaction he got from other people, such as fear, victimization, inadequacy, and criticism. You can imagine the types of friends with whom he associated.

Often people with this flaw tend to lump all their emotions into one category. They don't have the ability to sort through and distinguish between annoyance, frustration, irritation, and anger. They are just upset. From upset they go to raging indignation. Don't argue with them about it either. They can't tell the difference.

Smash the Computer!

Just before I started writing this chapter my computer crashed. Actually our oldest of five boys wanted to set up the new monitor for me. He pulled the old one off and plugged in the new one without shutting down the machine. Presto! The hard drive was vacuumed out. Entire directories were turned into files. Megs of data were lost. Most of my programs wouldn't run, especially the older ones. I spent the next sixteen waking hours on support lines talking with troubleshooters. Some of them droned out recommendations that I format the drive and use the backup disks. There was a slight problem with my backups, so I couldn't do it.

I decided I would remain calm because, after all, I was writing a chapter on raging indignation. I knew what to do. The start of most rage attacks is a stupid event. It could be any stupid event as long as we believe that we shouldn't have to put up with it. That is annoyance, in the early stages. After a few hours I was livid, and it was getting worse. At least this book and some others

> When angry, count four; when very angry, swear.
> —MARK TWAIN

I wrote weren't lost. But all of my beautiful slide and multimedia presentations were in cyberspace. And the fury was mounting. I had long since passed the stage of frustration. Frustration is the unwillingness to give up in spite of persistent failure. I had that one down pat. At least I had the failure part perfected.

I was just about to throw the computer out the window of my office when my wife called to remind me that we had to attend a first Communion party for a little boy. A great example I would have been, throwing the computer out the window and then driving over to a church function.

I let it go for a bit and cooled off. My wife laughed and I realized even the crash had a purpose. It got me in touch with the feelings I needed to describe in this chapter. I reorganized it and got back to work.

We all have fuses. We have to learn how to make them longer. Rage-aholics hate to let anything cool off. Staying heated and intense is a way for them to feel normal. Worse yet, they hate to wait for a long fuse to burn. The explosion is the thing that makes them feel alive.

I am convinced that there are male hormones involved here at some primitive level. Watch women negotiate with children, and watch men. Generally the men have much shorter fuses. Not that women can't be rage-aholics. There are many who are. Said one of my patients, characterizing her mother's rage, "Mom starts acting like a frustrated man." There may be some wisdom in that.

You may wonder where all the pent-up rage comes from. First of all rage is about as pent up as vomit. A raging person is different from someone who occasionally blows off steam out of frustration, anger, or bitterness. Raging indignation is never pent up; it is the continuous use of explosive anger to deal with everyday situations. It is blowing a fuse way before anyone else does. It comes from learning that anger and rage are a solution. Most often the raging indignant have been abused as children and had role models that blew their tops often and for no good reason.

Second, people who have pent-up anger and blow off now and then have usually learned how to suppress their anger. They may have grown up in a family where keeping a lid on it was the social norm. Emotions were not to be shown, much like the Windsors of England. The implied message is, "We are better than those highly emotional types. We control ourselves." Bully for you. I prefer to give ulcers rather than get them.

Remember, most of our patterns are based in our early relationships. They are not just learned but also hardwired in. You may come from a family that very easily learns to keep emotions stuffed, but God may have created you with a bit more expressiveness than your parents would like. When you get out of their household you may overcompensate a bit. That's not raging indignation even if it is frowned upon by your relatives who control themselves. With Italians it is the other way. You grow up and leave the house and realize you don't have to show as many feelings outside as you did inside the house.

As Sensual as Velcro

Others get stuck on our rage too, since our heartfelt passions are easily transferred. Go to a sporting event or a concert and watch masses of people respond together. Watch a workplace where people are arguing passionately about something. Chances are people will take sides. Emotions are sticky. When you touch them they hang on to you. Most of us see an emotion in someone else and try it on like a piece of clothing. We watch movies or hear stories and try to feel the feelings. It's fun to be compassionate.

Rage is like wearing Velcro. Touch it and you're stuck. It is a visceral reaction that has gone out of control. We intuitively know how to keep a safe distance from people who are raging. Most of us try to suppress our anger and distance ourselves from it. The closer we get to the source of the anger the more we see its power.

There are those who love to stoke the flames, the "stokers." They like to see people fired up. They have the character flaw but express it through others. They are as attached to raging indignation as the rage-aholic but feel more dignified fanning the flames of indignation in others. They light the flare. Once it ignites it burns on its own.

Statutory Violence

Stokers and the raging indignant both secretly believe that they are communicating with you when you are being battered. They practice what I call statutory violence. That is violence condoned or sanctioned by the rule that survival requires control. Get people to do it your way. They basically trust that most people will be persuaded by violence. They believe the experiences of violence are a valid way of treating others. Most of them have been battered and abused in their past. Anger is a way to deal with life.

The use of statutory violence is perfectly acceptable to protect society. We go to war to defend ourselves when we are attacked as a nation. It was General Patton who in effect said that the goal of the attack is to create intense fear in the enemy. The faster you can mobilize to full-strike force and inflict it on the opponent, the faster the battle will be resolved. In everyday life the problem is you are not at war but at work, school, or at home—or on the street—when it occurs.

I was in New York and a gang of young thugs was walking down the street. They were cutting up and acting like they were really tough, pushing people aside. They walked into a neighborhood on the East Side and got halfway down the block. Soon they were surrounded by another gang and the riot began. I watched in disbelief. It was like Attila the Hun meeting Genghis Khan. Both groups thought they were soldiers in a private military. Sometimes episodes likes this are racially motivated. Frequently, though, these fools are attacking members of their own ethnic group. That was years ago. We've progressed to militia groups now. Don't get me wrong, this is not a new phenomenon. We've had the Klan, Nazi socialists, and witch burning in the past. The character flaw has been around for millennia. It has many masks but reflects similar behaviors.

> **Men often make up in wrath what they want in reason.**
> **—WILLIAM ROUNSEVILLE ALGER**

There is far more power than we imagine hidden within the depths of raging indignation. Often it taps into discontent that is simmering below the surface of society. The problem is that raging indignation is not the solution to these problems—tolerance, peacefulness, and love are. They are not tried because of the intense fear that grips the raging indignant.

People who are afraid believe that they have the right to destroy things. Watch a little child who is afraid. Even one who never breaks a toy can be driven to destruction through fear.

Short Fuses, Hair Triggers, and the Lure of Violent Reaction

Most of us kindle before we burn. We all have a point at which the fire burns on its own. Most of us also have buttons that can be pushed to stoke us on and increase the heat. Our friends and family know what our buttons are. It's inevitable if you live with someone long enough he or she will learn how to push your buttons. But they are *your* buttons. It is your responsibility to disconnect them when they are causing problems.

I have seen some of my friends and colleagues mature and let go or lengthen their short fuses. Often it takes a lot of work to learn how to let things simmer and not overheat. When you are used to being a human keg of powder, everything else is less dramatic. It's hard to give up being outrageous and aggravating to others. Would you settle for being a fizzle rather than a cherry bomb?

Obscuring the Apparent

As a resident physician, I got to see all sorts of people who were pulled off the streets, rooftops, and bridges of New York City. The violently agitated were brought into the emergency room at Kings County Hospital. This is the largest hospital in New York City. The psychiatric emergency room was one of the busiest in the world.

Frequently two or three officers accompanied a poor soul who was psychotic and hallucinating. When I asked the patient how long he had been hearing voices, I would get a startled reaction. What was so obvious to me was a deep dark secret to the patient. Often patients were relieved because they had met someone who knew, who understood.

Most of the raging indignant and their partners in chaos, the stokers, are not psychotic. In fact they are using anger and indignation the way a drug addict uses a drug. They want to be revved up and feel normal. They may actually feel calmer after going ballistic. They love the excitement and the danger. They feel in control. But they don't want you to understand their secrets.

THE SECRETS OF THE RAGING INDIGNANT

- They know that they are unbalanced
- A button has been pushed and they hurt
- They feel weak
- Old issues or patterns aren't dead and are still causing problems
- They feel as ugly as they are acting
- They fear that you might be better than them

They know that they are unbalanced. You may call them wacky or off their rocker. Call them anything you want. As soon as you let them know that you think they are out of control or out of balance, you have taken some of their power away. Be careful. They may get angrier because you know this secret. They struggle desperately to pretend they are normal.

A button has been pushed and they hurt. They are using anger to medicate that ache within them. Even a little reaction to a small problem can escalate or develop into a raging pattern of behavior.

They feel weak. They are using anger to express a lack of strength or worse yet to reveal a place where strength is desperately needed.

> The worst-tempered people I've ever met were people who knew they were wrong.
> —WILSON MIZNER

Old issues or patterns aren't dead and are still causing problems. The roots may be unconscious patterns, the substance of which is complicated and interconnected with other issues from childhood.

They feel as ugly as they are acting. The most frequent positive comment I have had from patients with disfiguring burns is that at least their scars were on the outside and could be dealt with up front. The raging indignant and the stokers use anger to cover their emotional scars.

They fear that you might be better than they are. What they say to themselves is different, though. "If I am better than others it is my right to abuse them." Then, with twisted logic, they say, "If I have been able to abuse you, then I must be better than you." This is classically the bitter fruit of child abuse.

Battered Brides and Shattered Promises

Spouses who are filled with rage often try to make their partner the villain. It is easier to strike a bad guy, someone repugnant and sinister, than it is to hit someone you have promised your life to. The raging indignant try hard to make a villain of you so that they can strike you with cause. They have to justify not keeping the promises they have made.

Here is what they do. First a spouse looks to find character flaws in his or her partner. Usually this is done by finding what I called the "other half of the pair." Couples frequently have paired flaws. Raging indignation, for instance, pairs up well with victim syndrome or inadequacy. Then this person looks to keep a tally on the flaws and show how, if the partner didn't have the flaw, he or she wouldn't go into such violent reaction. Actually this person's rage is more often the trigger for the partner's flaws.

These individuals look to make villains out of others in order to have a focus for their anger. It is sick. And it is like playing with fire. They eventually burn themselves, but not before they have hurt someone they are in a relationship with and have vowed to honor and protect.

The raging indignant fight differently. They are prone to sneak attacks or an ambush with an apology offered at the end to atone.

Not too infrequently the apology is accompanied by an explanation for what was done wrong to get them so upset. They didn't mean it, but because of what you did they had an emotional spasm. It was unexpected and out of their control. "I'm sorry you made me do that to you. You should be more careful next time."

I don't buy this. After years of listening to patients who did this I came to realize that most of them were secretly planning on exploding when it was convenient. So much for this alleged spontaneity and lack of control. If you recall, the gremlins in the movie by that name planned to eat after midnight. They set it up. They wanted to be gremlins.

Descendants of the Damaged

Raging indignation really has a devastating effect on children even when it is experienced on TV. You know it. The behavioral scientists know it. It's just that the networks aren't sure. Those little central nervous systems are primed for taking in the volumes of information that the networks make available, including every deviation from the norm—scores of murders, rapes, and assaults. If you are not doing something about it you are a stoker. Learn to turn off the TV and make your children read. If not they will start to believe that it is quite all right to explode like a volcano.

WHAT TO DO WITH INDIGNATION WHEN YOU ENCOUNTER IT IN OTHERS

- Create a safety zone
- Don't bother to argue with insanity
- Confront the behavior firmly
- Look for the secret or fear

- Set up a time-out cue if they are willing
- Make sure they suffer the consequences
- Remove yourself as a target

Creating a safety zone is crucial. We used to keep a certain distance from really agitated patients and leave a way out of the room for the doctor and the patient. When a person is addicted to being right and arguing, you know that you have crossed a boundary. When a person is in raging indignation you are not safe unless you are out of the zone of danger. That's more than just a boundary. It's a zone. Sometimes it's physical. Sometimes it is an emotional zone. Some of my patients did much better when they went away to school. They had to go very far enough away to be safe. If the rage-aholic is prone to physical abuse it may mean leaving the premises. It may mean seeking shelter. But it always means getting far enough away that you won't get hurt.

Don't bother to argue with insanity. You can't reason with it, nor can you share your feelings. Insanity is an equal-opportunity destroyer. Whoever gets in its way is due for trouble. Recently, I watched a guy fly down an interstate highway after another car. These two clowns were yelling at each other weaving in and out of traffic. They were both crazy. Years ago at worst it would have come to a fistfight. Now it becomes a bloodbath.

Confront angry behavior firmly. You should confront the behavior and not the person. I had an old Scottish boss when I worked as a respiratory therapist in college. I think he enjoyed my anger and loved to say, "Laddie, you're a bright boy and I know it, but that's a damn stupid behavior and I could fire you for it." In the ER we used to make a point of trying to develop some rapport with agitated people before we confronted the behavior. Make sure you are in a safety zone first, though, or you could be in trouble. It is ethical to oppose the raging indignant and to confront the stoker. Do so with a certain amount of coolness and restraint. You are trying to care for yourself first, not fix them.

The raging indignant hate to be told that they are out of control. They resent the fact that you can see through their behavior. That is the last thing that they want to hear. Point out what is wrong with the behavior, not them. An old bag lady pulled a butcher's knife on me at the Kings County Hospital ER. I rang the secret buzzer and the hospital police officer turned it off three times before he came in to tell me not to keep bumping the buzzer. That gave me ample opportunity to try and defuse the patient's rage. I said to her, "When you wave that knife around, it scares the crap out of me. Did you know that? This is a hospital and you can't be causing the doctors to mess their shorts now, so put it down." She laughed long enough for the guards to grab her.

Look for the secret. You need to know it in order to be more effective with the raging indignant. I've watched David Toma, the original antidrug crusader, do this with hundreds of enraged teenagers. Many of them wanted to fight with him onstage. They thought that they were going to take him out! They were tough kids who ranted and raved at him. Toma got right in their faces and nailed their secrets. They collapsed like little wounded children and sought help. He knew that most of the raging indignant were hurt and feeling weak and vulnerable.

If you have a relationship with someone who is prone to this character defect, **set up a time-out**. It is a device you use for little children and it works well here. That's probably because the rage-aholic has regressed to around six years of age emotionally. Maybe that's why so many rage-aholics find women who can nurture and mother them. A temper tantrum in a grown-up is far more dangerous than one in a child.

If you have developed a plan to deal with a raging indignant, **make sure he or she suffers consequences.** There is no change with this character defect without some suffering. Patients would tell me, "The next time he hits me I am leaving or filing for divorce."

You must be ready to carry it out. Idle threats serve to inflame the raging indignant's appetite for violence.

If all else fails, completely remove yourself as a target. Sometimes the only intelligent thing to do is to get out of the range of rage. Shelter yourself from its sphere of influence.

Passionate Restraint

I told a young man, Sam, who prided himself on his violence, that he was at his weakest when he was unrestrained. He thought I was kidding. "Doc, when I'm pissed, when I am really agitated, others know how powerful I really am." He was a large-framed sanitation worker who liked throwing things, and sometimes people, around.

The philosopher Aristotle addressed this issue long ago when he wrote, "Anybody can become angry—that is easy; but to be angry with the right person, and to the right degree, and at the right time, and for the right purpose, and in the right way—that is not within everybody's power and is not easy."

Sam didn't know when and how to become angry. He was creating chaos everywhere, in his relationships, work, and social life. He was like a guy on steroids without the drugs. Inside he was an inadequate little boy, wanting approval from everyone, especially his abusive father, who wanted him to be tough so that he would survive. Thank God he liked to race cars, because it gave me a hook.

"What has more power, a gallon of racing fuel in the engine of your finely tuned race car, or a bucket of that fuel and a cigarette lighter?" I asked.

"Same power, Doc, just used differently," said Sam.

He was being sarcastic with me, so I asked him to explain the differences in results. After listening to his own ramblings for a while, he started to get the picture. Being able to control the energy of the explosions and harness it was what made an engine powerful. He was certain that I wanted him to learn how to be sweet and gentle. I assured him that he didn't have to go that far.

We settled on cool, restrained, and powerful, a kind of James Bond attitude. If you suffer from raging indignation, you have a choice to make: restrained power or loss of control. You have a choice to dissipate your energy in aggression or become passionate through restraint. The choice is yours. Here's what my patient decided to do.

HOW TO RID YOURSELF OF THE CHARACTER FLAW

• Exhale slowly

• Do a deathbed contrast

• See the anger as chains

• Empty the garbage

• Focus on what you love

Exhale slowly. I thought this was simplistic when my patient suggested that it was the first step in calming down. He explained that while watching guys fight he noticed that the more violent they were going to be, the deeper they breathed and the faster they blew it out. He had thrown the javelin and discus and learned about being explosive. I had to agree with him. Taking a slow middle-sized breath into your belly and slowly exhaling shuts down some of the fight-or-flight reaction.

Do a deathbed contrast. I was even more impressed with his insight when he told me what else he was going to do. He had been at his grandfather's side when he died. A cousin had come to visit Grandpa after a long period of separation. My patient couldn't understand why his grandfather had forgiven the man. He remembered his grandfather saying, "From here, at the end of my life the whole stupid situation doesn't seem so big."

This second step was to pause and look at the situation from where he was, then contrast it with the image of himself on his deathbed. He tried to see if the matter was of any importance from there. If it was, he would give himself permission to fight tenaciously, but in a way that was restrained enough to give him good results. If not he was going to blow it off. He knew his grandfather was right. He also knew that most of what he got angry about was meaningless.

His next step was to **see the anger that persisted as chains,** binding his power and sapping his strength. The picture in his mind was that of Samson in the temple. He believed that real strength comes from God. If he gave himself some time, time for his hair to grow, he could use the chains rather than be bound by them.

The chains that anger represents are anchored to strong needs. He decided that when he found himself bound by them he would look to see what secret would unlock the chains.

Empty the garbage. "If your garbage isn't disposed of regularly your whole neighborhood begins to stink." He was right.

His last step surprised me. **Focus on what you love**. Here was a guy who was afraid I was going to try to convince him that he had to be sweet and gentle, talking to me about a focus on love.

The most remarkable thing that happens to a person who gives up the right to raging indignation is that he finds profound peace. It is associated with enormous power and restrained passion. A sense of capability and calm competence take over. If you don't give up the right to raging indignation, you get stuck in vengeance. That will bring on the next level of character flaw: Fixing Blame and Nurturing Resentments.

Fixing Blame and Nurturing Resentments

HOW DO YOU KNOW IF YOU ARE *FIXING BLAME AND NURTURING RESENTMENTS?*

1. Do you believe that revenge is a civil right?

2. When caught doing something wrong, do you point out how other people are to blame?

3. Do you blame others so that you won't be judged?

4. Do you try to take the focus off yourself by blaming others?

5. Do you blame others so that you will get recognized?

6. Do you enjoy rejecting others?

7. Do you hold on to past grievances long after they are forgotten by others?

8. Do you try to avoid accountability when things go wrong?

9. Does payback feel like justice to you?

10. Do you usually consider yourself innocent?

11. When you can't sort your personal affairs, do you look for a scapegoat?

12. Do you have a marriage made in hell, by the other person?

13. Do you protect your personal rights over your personal responsibility?

14. Do you use the excuse "Everybody else was doing it"?

15. Do you justify things by saying the other person "made me do it"?

16. Do you start sentences with words like "You make me feel so . . . "?

17. Do you accept people with conditions?

18. Do you whine?

19. When there is a problem in a relationship, do you look to see what's wrong with the other person first?

Imagine the scene in hell: Don Corleone meets the Hatfields and McCoys. What would they have in common to talk about? You guessed it, resentment and vengeance. The Hatfields and McCoys were the nineteenth-century archetype of resentment and vengeance. Don Corleone of *The Godfather* is the Hollywood version.

Every culture has its belief that to avenge is noble. I have a nineteenth-century Japanese lithograph in my office showing Yamasaburo, a young samurai, going off to avenge the death of his father. He was a noble character whose father had been unjustly murdered. It was his duty to avenge the death.

So how does avenging, which so often is portrayed as noble, get debased into a character flaw?

The boy avenging his father's unjust death is ridding society of a tyrant. That is quite noble. In most cases it is character at work.

However, if the noble quality of vengeance for justice's sake turns into revenge or spite for its own sake, there is a problem. We all know those venom-spitting hypocrites who want to pay back people who have harmed them.

Payback Is a B . . .

Anna Maria, a mother of two, came into my office complaining that she was having anxiety attacks and insomnia. "It's his fault. The bastard has ruined my life," she said. "I have been punishing him for years. He had an affair. I used it against him to make him miserable. We stayed together for the kids. At least he did. I stayed together to torture him. If I divorced him he would be free. Then what would I do with all this pent-up resentment?"

"It doesn't seem too pent up to me," I suggested.

"Look, Doc, I have tried to make him suffer. I get him to the point where I think he is miserable. Then I check to see how I feel. I don't feel any better. In fact I still feel bad, maybe just a little bit worse than he does. So I work at making him even more miserable. I have gone from a hurt young lady to a miserable old bitch. And he still hasn't been hurt enough."

Finally her soul had had enough. She had multiple panic attack symptoms, but medications hadn't worked. The symptoms left her when she started to care for him and feel forgiveness. It was time for her to stop using blame and resentment. She was stewing in her own spite.

Why Is Blame Useful?

Blame at first seems to be just. It is a way of holding people accountable. Little children all learn to tattletale when it serves their needs. It is a way of avoiding punishment for something we haven't done. What makes it a character flaw is when it is used to hurt the innocent so we can avoid punishment for something we have done.

Usually we fear reprisal or punishment, so we try to "cover our own asses." Sometimes, however, we just want to elevate ourselves in the eyes of others.

Blame surfaces anytime you have adolescent thinking. A colleague of mine at NYU used to say that adolescence should be a diagnosis, especially if you are an adult acting like one. It should have a special name like adult adolescent thinking disorder. You know the type, always justifying what they did wrong by blaming someone else. They don't want responsibility when things go wrong, yet they always seek recognition when things go right. Blame is a way for them to salvage self-esteem because they only feel good when things go right. "It's not my fault" is one of their mantras. Being at fault feels threatening and dangerous, perhaps because at some time in the past it actually was. They go into an emotional cave-in whenever something goes wrong.

These are the people who beg forgiveness when they do something wrong and yet criticize and punish others for the same offenses.

Here is another mantra: "I wouldn't have had to do anything dishonest if they hadn't . . ." That was almost an exact quote from a politician on TV. I don't expect that from my eight-year-old, but he tries it at times. I certainly don't accept it from elected officials. We must expect people to act like adults and hold them accountable.

How Did It Get Started?

The blame game starts like any of the games we play. We decide what winning is, then we do everything we can to get there. When failure occurs blame is the best way to cope. Then we stack the ill will and anger and create resentment, or anger that keeps seething over time. We take a mixture of ambition and fear, mix it with a little jealousy and envy. Then we throw in some dishonesty and addicted to being right and we have spite stew.

Jealousy is described as being fearful or wary of being supplanted; apprehensive of losing affection or position. Envy on the other hand is a feeling of discontent and resentment aroused by the desire for the possessions or qualities of another. So we either want the affection of others or the stuff that others have. When we can't get them, we blame someone else for our failings. Since jealousy and envy are never really satisfied, chronic blamers are always failing to get what they need. They continuously have to blame and feel resentment.

There are many methods for blaming. For example, the politician cited above tried to excuse himself by pointing out the alleged greater sin in others. He was trying to take the focus off himself and place it on someone else. Sometimes the sophisticated blamer will only have to raise an eyebrow. I had a friend who used to say "Oh really?" with a tone that meant "You're acting like an idiot and are wrong to think like that." Look around where you are and listen to someone whine. You will be given a lesson in how to resent or blame.

In the Bible it says, "Judge not and you shall not be judged. Condemn not and you shall not be condemned." Most of the time we find blamers avoiding being judged rather than not judging others. A smart blamer won't judge others directly. He'll get you to judge others. He will graciously point out what is wrong. Then he will immediately look to duck and cover his butt by pointing out that it is not his fault.

I find it especially difficult to listen to highly competent individuals who have been reduced to whining and complaining. If they were accountable and focused on results, rather than blame, they would get a lot more done. These people are addicted to praise and pride. They hope desperately to be validated by others in order to salvage their self-esteem. At least they think so. I would be ashamed to whine that loudly.

There is no real satisfaction in blaming, just bitterness. Blame creates a tower of hurt when all the things that we resent get stacked up. You know the "stackers." They have this habit of recalling two or three other episodes to blame you for, when they find fault. They create a kind of pancake effect. Month after month they pile up separate instances of resentment and anger. They create a chain of negative emotions that cascades to the worst hurt in the stack. It is amazing to see. They explode in rage, because they are seething with resentment. You may have known people who have laundry lists of past bad experiences that they dredge up whenever convenient.

More times than not the explosions are based on resentments that were triggered by really insignificant events. They catch us off guard. That is one of those universal flags that go up to remind you that you are dealing with a character flaw. Watch someone take a minor event and add it to a lifetime of accumulated hurts. You can understand why he or she is "fed up and can't take it anymore."

Sometimes it's not stacked from the same source. It is easier to justify the blame when you have multiple episodes from the same person. Fool me once, shame on you. Fool me twice, shame on me. Fool me thrice and blame on thee, and better yet resentment.

If you listen to blamers talk about their childhoods, you'll soon realize that they grew up in a punishing environment not geared to solutions but to fixing blame. They take a strategy that helped them survive their childhood and then try to make it work in the adult world, where they constantly fear having their pride damaged.

There is false pride in people who blame and resent. By false pride I mean pride used to defend a defect in character. Just look at the ones near you who do it. You will see fear mixed with ambition and wounded pride. When blamers try for revenge it usually backfires. Vengeance is dangerous. There is an old saying that if you're going to seek revenge, dig two graves.

How to Identify the Person Who Is Digging Two Graves

I like to listen to the tone blamers use when they whine to me. I am convinced that their motto is "Fix the blame, not the problem." Most of the time I aggravate them by asking the terrible question, "So how are you going to make the situation better?" They can't answer. They don't believe that they are in control. Making the situation better is not the point. Taking the focus off their own defects and inadequacies is the goal.

Look at the following issues:

- Blame needs a scapegoat
- Blame and resentment is looking for praise even though things have failed
- Blame and resentment tries to move the focus to others
- Blame and resentment thrives on rejection
- Blame and resentment is the opposite of forgiveness
- Blame and resentment believes people are victims and aren't in control
- Blame and resentment is not looking for solutions

Blame needs a scapegoat. Scapegoats are useful for taking the focus off the real problem. Families will develop scapegoats, such as problem children, so that no one notices the other real problems like marital discord. Politicians scapegoat each other so no one notices the real agenda of control and manipulation.

Blame and resentment is looking for praise even though things have failed. When self-esteem is so tightly related to winning or losing, success or failure, then a blamer looks for praise rather than responsibility. It doesn't matter to the blamer if things have gone wrong. "Give me recognition or give me death!"

Blame and resentment tries to move the focus to others. Shift the focus, move the attention, and then get others to blame someone else. Have you ever listened to someone answer a question with an unrelated topic? Like the Sunday talking heads from Washington. They don't answer questions, they simply shift the focus and imply blame.

Blame and resentment thrives on rejection. Funny as it may seem, blamers thrive in an environment where someone is going to get rejected. God forbid it should be them. In fact they will help you decide who to reject and where to focus the rejection.

Blame and resentment is the opposite of forgiveness. How many times should a person with this character flaw blame? Seventy times seven, to paraphrase Jesus' advice on forgiveness. There can never be too much blame if it can inflate the ego. More is better.

Blame and resentment believes people are victims and aren't in control. Haven't you noticed how convenient the excuses are from people who blame? They enjoy playing victim and pretend they have no control.

Blame and resentment is not looking for solutions. It is looking simply to make sure someone is scapegoated. Results don't matter. In fact you have to wonder if bad results are really cherished because blamers gloat over failure when they can blame someone for it.

The character defect of blame develops into chronic resentment almost imperceptibly. It just sort of happens. We don't notice where it began, because we are in denial that we use it. That is why it is so important to look at what the resentment represents.

Mirror, Mirror on the Wall

What you may really be seeing is a lot more complicated than it appears at first glance. Resentment means holding a grudge, even after the matter has apparently been settled, because you believe you were harmed. It is holding on to those lingering hard feelings even after the incident is long over. It may look as if little issues trigger the resentment. The amount of energy expended is a clue, however, that it's something bigger. The attacks, the tirades, and the tantrums all point to deeper issues. Blame is the mask of distraction used to divert your attention to something else. Blame is the great mirror to the soul. The life energy is in a Gordion knot. Watch what a person is constantly blaming others for and you will get a glimpse of what his or her life's energy is consumed with.

- Blame and resentment is searching for accountability
- Blame and resentment is fear of accountability
- Blame and resentment is the way to get the heat off yourself
- Blame and resentment is the universal desire to be innocent
- Blame and resentment is an attempt to look good, to save face, self-esteem
- Blame and resentment is the way to split people into groups, divide and conquer
- Resentment is trying to stack old pain, sort things out
- Blame and resentment wants to do what was done to him or her—it feels like justice
- Blame and resentment wants vengeance—punishment

Who's responsible here? We should be teaching accountability in every area of our lives. In business we do it as a matter of course through bookkeeping and inventory. In our schools we also try. Children are taught to clean up after themselves, and hopefully teachers are still trying to mete out fair punishment for misbehavior. It is perfectly fine to blame people for things they did wrong and hold them accountable.

The great teachers of accountability are parents. It is a job that never ends. As long as there are parents, there will be children trying to get away with something. It will always be our duty to teach the next generation how to be accountable, especially if the punishment fits the crime.

Blame and resentment is fear of accountability: It ain't me, babe. For some, accountability is a difficult lesson to teach because they haven't learned it themselves. I heard on the news the other day that a burglar brought his son to "work" with him because he couldn't find day care for the little child. The father was arrested for breaking and entering. Hopefully he was trying to teach his child that stealing was wrong. Getting caught was how he was going to teach accountability to his son. You doubt it too?

Blame is the way to get the heat off yourself. More likely the burglar-dad will blame the police or the burglar-alarm system or some other person for his getting caught. This foolish, felonious father will miss the opportunity to teach a lesson he needs to learn. He will use blame to get the heat off himself. This is an all too common occurrence when children are afraid of being physically hurt if they are to blame. I can remember a few times that my sister blamed me for something. She was afraid of the "wooden spoon." I was the kind of kid who eventually got used to it and didn't care.

We all would like to be innocent or undo the things we did wrong. The adolescent adult thinks that the appropriate way of maintaining innocence is either to blame others or to have a "do-over."

Faulting someone else doesn't make you innocent no matter how well you place the blame. The truth is still truth.

I am as pretty as I look, not as I feel. Blaming others is a way of maintaining self-esteem by looking good in the eyes of others. The truth is that self-esteem comes only from your own view of yourself and not from the opinions of others. Someone else's opinion of me is not self-esteem. It's just "steam" or hot air.

Here are two goofy beliefs associated with low self-esteem in blamers: "If I am not at fault then I am good. If I am not at fault and good, then I am a worthy individual." Often when things have gone very wrong in relationships we feel guilty and ashamed. Everybody knows a divorcee who has had to deal with shame. Blaming the other person feels as right as rain. It comes as naturally as breathing. I've only seen a couple of those so-called dignified divorces where the couple splits up without blame and without resentment. They were fun to watch. In both couples one partner was a minister. In retrospect I think they were putting on an act for the sake of their congregations. One of them was definitely lying to look "spiritual."

Divide and conquer. Blame and resentment is a character flaw that splits people into groups. The good and the bad are created to help the blamer cope with a hostile world. Since the days of Machiavelli even politicians have admitted that they do this. Without getting fancy with the pathology involved, let me remind you that it is sick to keep splintering people into groups to weaken them.

We have a national movement called diversity. The idea is to respect everyone's diversity. That's the healthy side of this process. Too often, though, people are split into groups so that each group knows who to hate. Splitting and blaming is how it is done. Create enough resentments in a group and you can weaken it. We are not strong as a society because of our diversity but in spite of it. We are strong because of our unity. We are rich because of our diversity.

I'm so confused about what went wrong. Often blame and resentment is the only tool that an individual has to sort things out. When things don't go well it is easy to figure out what went wrong. Then you assign blame, which is easier to do than it is to learn from what went wrong. Learning from our mistakes requires an open and honest view.

We are taught at an early age to stop after we fail at something and to review what went wrong so we don't have to make the same mistake again. The problem is that some people use that as a time to lump new disappointments with the old. It is a pause for resentment.

"Once again I have been shown that women are unpredictable and overly emotional," said an accountant whose relationship was on the rocks over something he had done. He had gone back and sorted through the relationship. Not wanting anything to be his fault he automatically blamed his emotional girlfriend. To further compound the problem he lumped her "emotional behavior" into the same category with his previous failed relationships. You should have heard him try to explain to me what "emotional behavior" was. "All women have it, Doc. You know what I mean."

I didn't. He couldn't explain it too well either. Thank God he couldn't because it was the key to his seeing how he always blamed the ladies for his crass and irritating behavior.

It feels like justice to me! "I just wanted him to hurt like I hurt," the wife of an alcoholic said to me. She had been going around to bars drinking and picking up men to punish her husband for his drinking. Now she was signing a consent form for HIV testing. She was terrified.

She started out to punish her husband. At first it felt like justice. She hadn't counted on the fact that she was a sex addict. She didn't expect sex with strangers to have a soothing effect on her the way the alcohol did on him. The problem was that once was not enough. No matter how often she went out, she wanted more. What started out as a way to take care of her feelings of resentment, while creating justice, became a personal nightmare of addiction and disease. She learned the hard way that his was a disease too. In her attempts to punish him she punished herself and everyone close to her.

Blame and resentment wants punishment. The character flaw thrives on vengeance. A chemist who was angry with his wife over her excessive spending came to my office to discuss his anxiety. He had been plotting all sorts of vicious little surprises for her. He sabotaged her car so she couldn't go shopping. He canceled credit cards, changed bank accounts, and sometimes refused the UPS deliveries from the TV shopping networks. He was actually angry with his mother, who had also been a shop-aholic.

During one session he sat and justified all his devious schemes. "Vengeance is sweet, Dr. T," he said with a sarcastic tone.

" 'Vengeance is mine,' sayeth the Lord," I responded, mirroring his sarcasm.

"Well I ripped that page out of my Bible," he shot back.

"It's time to stop playing God. You're re-creating hell and it's the cause of your anxiety."

Like the chemist, you may as well get used to the idea: this character flaw will always make you feel like you have the right to punish someone else. You may have that right. You might be justified. Key word "might." Just remember this character flaw is linked to martyr syndrome, which will never let you believe that you have punished the other person enough. Martyrs feel justified in their vengeance but never satisfied.

Marriages Made in Hell

Marriages are made in heaven, right? After all the couples I've seen, I'm not too sure. I know that most of the time they are not made down here on earth. When blame and its cargo, resentment, infect a marriage it becomes fertile grounds for constant conflict. It is a marriage made in hell.

When I came through residency training, the focus in therapy was almost always the individual. We discussed rights, such as the right to have the feelings that you have. We also focused on beliefs. Most of the time we focused on traumas from the past and how they affect present-day behavior.

Little by little the fields of couples therapy and family therapy emerged to fill the gaps in our treatment repertoire. The biggest gap as I saw it was the need to focus couples away from their individual rights. Good marriages are not made of individuals. Good marriages are made of two becoming spiritually united as one. I know it sounds old-fashioned, but it takes sacrifice, commitment, and responsible action to make a marriage strong. The focus on individual rights breeds discontent, blame, and resentments. Focusing on responsibilities, duties, and roles helps to clarify misunderstandings that lead to blame.

I am not naive enough to think that relationships are easy if you follow a few simple rules. They can be very difficult. But when one of the partners blames and harbors intense resentments the relationship is often doomed. Good, long-lasting relationships require that we reduce our egos and release our character flaws.

A gentleman visited me prior to his retirement. He had endured years of being blamed for everything that went wrong in his relationship. The fact was that Tony, as I shall call him, was responsible for most of the acute crisis that occurred throughout the years. He knew it. The problem was that his wife did too and never let him forget it. She was a stacker and blamed him for everything. She would read him a list of what he did wrong. It served as her evening litany to him.

Finally he decided that he'd had enough and refused to agree with her on a minor issue. I hate to admit it but I encouraged him to refuse to accept responsibility for something that he hadn't done. She became enraged and in a fit of vengeance decided on divorce. I didn't count that as a successful outcome, but who knows.

When one partner resents, the other gets demonized. Patients who are unduly rebellious choose to act out even more, because they hate being blamed. "As long as I am being blamed for it I might as well do it."

We treat resentment as relatively innocuous. We believe that there is no great cause for alarm. "If I resent that person, I'll just avoid him" is what we tell ourselves. The problem is that it contaminates our thinking in other areas. We don't function as well as we could when we walk around with resentments.

Most of the time blamers use some pretty silly excuses. Here are some of the more ridiculous excuses I've heard:

- "She asked for it"
- "She made me do it"

- "He was going to cheat on me anyhow"
- "Everybody else was doing it"
- "He was mean to me"

The list could go on and on. If you are in a relationship with another person, the character flaws of the other person are reflected in you. How you handle their blaming and resentment is a reflection of what the flaw is doing to you on the inside. You have other flaws that balance out the blame and resentment.

Most spouses who are married to someone using resentment are well equipped to play with the character flaw of victimization. It is part of their game. They chose the person to be with in the relationship. They might not have done it consciously. It may have just been a marriage made in hell.

Children of the Blamed

There is an old saying that if you raise children with criticism and blame they will grow up to find fault. Sure they will. After all, they want to feel normal. Blaming is the most normal thing for some people. I love to watch little kids when you say, "We have a problem and I need help fixing it." Some children will immediately start to defend themselves. "I didn't do it. It's not my fault. By the way, what is the problem?"

Others, who have grown up in an environment where duty and responsibility are taught, want to know right away what they can do, how they can help.

Think about the long-term effect that blame has on a child's productivity and creativity. How does your blame and resentment affect your children? Have you heard parents who ask those really dumb questions or make those classic blaming statements?

- What's wrong with you?
- See what you made me do?
- You make me feel so . . . !
- Now look at what you've done!

The list could go on.

The worst-case scenario is resentment for your spouse or for the mother or father of your child. Blaming your spouse or your ex-spouse often causes your child to feel guilty and inadequate. A young engineer came to my office complaining of the feeling of inadequacy. I worked with her for a while and it became apparent that it was related to the tirades of blame and resentment launched against her father by her mother when she was young. She loved him deeply and part of her decided that there must be something wrong for her to love someone who was bad. She must basically be inadequate.

We use the same patterns that we have been taught. These are the models we use for relationships. We learn about blame and resentment at an early age. In my family, holding resentments was an Italian art form. It had to be done properly. My maternal grandmother was particularly good at it. You didn't just resent, you had to create drama. If you were really melodramatic you were creating opera. I guess the melodramatic types reading this didn't know that they had some Italian in them.

Easier to Forgive a Stranger

I was making rounds as a respiratory therapist, working my way through my undergraduate courses. I had a respiratory patient who was a psychiatrist. We used to talk for hours. I wanted to find out what it was like to be a psychiatrist and he was more than willing to tell me.

During one conversation I mentioned that I was angry with my mother and feeling guilty about it. He said, "It is much easier to forgive a stranger than a family member." I thought that was odd, but in retrospect I decided he was right. There is no history with the stranger. It is harder to have stacks of small hurts piling up into resentment. There is always more pathology when a person holds resentments against a stranger. In other words the person who is resentful against someone who cuts him off in traffic is far sicker than a son who resents something his mother has done.

Still it feels wrong to hold resentments against those you love.

Resentment and Moral Hypocrisy

Too often resentment is harbored by intellectual and emotional snobs. You know the type. They are addicted to being right and they are especially right about their feelings. Life might be simpler if all we had to do was to respond to feelings, but that's not how things work. We have intuition, which gives us our hunches, sensation, which gives us our facts, and thinking, which gives us our ideas or judgments of the facts, our hunches, and our feelings.

Often resentments are based on our judgments, which are based on our feelings, which may or may not be based on sensation. I am deliberately spinning you around on this one because it is important to realize that burning resentments are rarely justified. The harder it is to make you feel seething resentment, the finer your character is. Most of the time we seethe with resentment because of pride, envy, and a whole host of character flaws that leave us believing we are better than others. Unless you are willing to look at seething resentment to discover where you need more humility, you are probably not making the world a better place.

Humility is the key because it is moral snobbery to think you have a right to resent, when you actually have a responsibility to be more humble and forgiving. It is intellectual snobbery to resent the ideas of others rather than be fascinated by them.

What to Do When You Are Assailed by Blame and Resentment

There are two basic rules that I use in relationships.

- Rule #1: When there is a problem in your relationship, change a character flaw in yourself
- Rule #2: If you discover the other person is to blame, reread rule #1

Here's the key to handling this flaw. Let's take a look at what to do with the person who is possessed by this flaw and who has decided to inflict it upon you.

- Don't stir the stew
- Practice acceptance
- Practice accountability
- Know each other's rules
- Recognize what your responsibility is and what it isn't
- Focus on your own behavior and character
- Forgive as you would a stranger

Don't stir the stew. When I was a kid there was a cesspool that overflowed at our house at the Jersey shore. When it was dug up I was overcome by curiosity. I got the longest stick I could find and then I stirred it up a bit. Soon I was overcome by the smell. It's like that with people who are possessed by this character flaw. You could try debating the person who is blaming you, but most of the time it is not about being right or wrong, it is about some other need, so why bother. It is better to:

Practice acceptance. Practicing acceptance requires an attitude that says in effect, "I will try to see how the human soul is operating through this character flaw of blame and resentment." The human soul operates even when we are using defenses that seem base and crude. Blame and resentment implies that there is still some work to be done.

Practicing acceptance appears to be harder than it is. Sometimes all it takes is listening for a few more minutes, trying to view things from the other person's perspective. In the long run it is the path of least resistance and is the more spiritually correct one. Over the short haul it is much easier to practice irritability and intolerance with blamers. It is even more exciting and dramatic to practice raging indignation with people who inflict seething resentment.

Practice accountability. More important, you need to set up accountability methods that work. Before holding someone accountable make sure you specifically define the behavior in question. Sometimes that means a chore list for your children. Or it may mean a phone log at work for your salespeople.

Know each other's rules. In relationships make sure that both sides understand the rules to be followed. Sometimes the problem is as simple as one side believing she "must be faithful" and the other side believing he "should be faithful." When the rules are different, the behaviors that break the rules are different. Thus we argue and blame.

Recognize what is and isn't your responsibility. If your rules or guidelines are set and the blame comes flying at you, stop and decide whether it is your responsibility or not. I personally feel that the best way to short-circuit someone who blames you is to quickly accept the responsibility for your part in it. Then move on. Most of the time people who are not possessed by the flaw will move on. If they want to whine and complain or continue to rant and rave, you are dealing with people who are stuck. They believe they have something to gain.

If not they wouldn't be stuck. Whatever it is they believe they deserve, it probably isn't your duty to give it to them. You need to move on too, but refuse to argue. A word of caution. Don't ever accept responsibility for something you didn't do. That would be dishonest. It may be grandiose as well, or you may be setting yourself up as a victim.

Focus on your own behavior and character. If you do have some responsibility in the situation, focus on your own behavior and your own character. All too often a couple will argue about something until one of the two accepts some responsibility, then the blame shifts. Now that person tries to get the other to accept responsibility too. The implied message is, "I'm a morally superior, enlightened, in tune, and karmically aligned dude." Or, "I'm a Christian who really practices his faith. Be like me, admit you're wrong too."

Next, the partners in this modern-day psychobabbling couple blame and judge each other. Each feels morally superior and guilty at the same time. That has to be better than just plain guilty, right? It's not better, just more complicated. It's blame masquerading as spiritual enlightenment.

Forgive as you would a stranger. Remember what the psychiatrist in the hospital told me: it is easier to forgive a stranger. How do you do that with someone you have a longtime relationship with? First of all you have to unstack the hurt. Focus only on the one incident that just occurred. Unstacking the piles of garbage and focusing on the present moment is crucial.

We forgive strangers more easily, because we try not to attribute malicious motives to their behavior. We cut them a break in our own minds. You need to do the same thing with someone you love. Look for a motive that is self-serving and related to fear. They wouldn't attack if they weren't afraid of something. The people in your life who do stupid things, and that may be everybody, need to be held accountable. They don't need hatred or resentment. They need acceptance and accountability.

Forgiveness has another advantage. Generally there is a thread of truth running through your stacked hurts. Those painful incidents that are the basis of your resentments are glued together. The glue that holds them together is your personal power. The more resentments you have, the more glue you are using to hold all that crap together. That means that your personal power is being sapped with each resentment.

Why Bother to Change? A Flood of Prosperity and Success!

Of all the character flaws, blaming is most intimately related to the issue of prosperity and success. More often than not when you release the right to blame others something dramatic occurs. You become more successful. I know it sounds strange, but I have seen it so often. The key to greater abundance and prosperity is often held in our ability to be accountable. The only thing standing between most of us and being accountable is the desire to blame others. When it goes, then all the excuses go. You've made room for abundance.

One of my patients who was an old recovering alcoholic had an approach to getting rid of resentments that was very practical. Treat it like your hair. Keep cutting it back until it all falls out. I think it was a good simile for him because he was bald. For most of us it is like shaving. Don't you ladies feel more beautiful after your legs are shaved?

Unless you get rid of the resentment completely, it will grow back again and again. That's not bad or good, just human nature. So shave it when it surfaces. And keep at it. Sometimes we gain insights that allow us to release the resentment completely. That's a noble goal. I recommend it, but I realize it's more likely that you will have to start over every day like the rest of us mere mortals.

It's also worth it to stop blaming because of what resentment does to your future. There is a simple process that I used with some patients. We would visualize the time line. That is a cluster of images reflecting how you view your past, present, and future. Usually the future is in a line running from you out to the front or off to the side. The close images are the near future and the farther images are the distant future.

Here is what we would do. We would create forgiveness in the past and then have it run through the time line. All the future images would get brighter and more exciting. That's what happens to the rest of your life when you let go of blame. It gets brighter and more exciting.

How to Shave Blame and Unglue Resentments

I wish this were easy. It is simple to do. It just has to be done constantly. Since character flaws are easier and more convenient than virtues, it may take a while for you to get the hang of this. It's like shaving. You do it quite easily now, but in the beginning it was more complicated.

You have to work on blame and resentment every time it shows up. As soon as you start to focus on the other person, stop and admit you're blaming. Responsibility is the main issue. You need to focus on what your responsibility is. Be accountable for what you have done. Focus only on your own part in the problem, unless the other person asks you to point out what is wrong. Then use the rule of three. I have a rule that I use in my nonprofessional relationships. I don't give people my opinion of their behavior unless they ask for it. When they ask for it three times, I give it to them.

It is better to focus on your side of the blame and treat the other person as blameless for the time being. That will keep you focused on your own stuff. After all, I hope you're reading this for you and not so that you can fix someone else in your life.

If you break down the release of blame and resentment you will find that forgiveness is the key.

- Stay with the individual incident
- Praise others and stop seeking approval
- Focus on your own character
- Practice charity and forgiveness

Every time you hear yourself whining and blaming someone for what went wrong, step back and look at yourself. **Stay with the individual episode** of resentment. Unstack the old hurts unless they are useful for protection. Most of the time they aren't, regardless of how you try to justify it. Take your power pack and deal with the individual episode. That will reduce resentment to blame. It is easier to deal with blame, because you can then focus on yourself. Next separate the person you blamed from their behavior. Keep the "who they are" and "what they did" separate. That will make it easier for you to deal with your blame.

Listen to the tones behind blame and resentment. As soon as you recognize how you do it, your whining can be a trigger to **praise others and stop seeking recognition.**

When I taught medical students how to interview, I would not let them criticize their fellows. I used to make them point out what was done right. They all knew where and how they had messed up. They needed to know what they were doing right to get comfortable with the process. If you are a blamer, then you don't naturally point out what is going right but look for what is going wrong. Change that today. It will shock your friends and associates.

Focus on your own character . Chances are you are trying to feel righteous by holding resentment. Clearly it doesn't work, so stop scapegoating and look for things that you can change in you. Remember, judge not.

Stop judging others. **Practice charity or love and forgiveness.** We had a drill that we did in group. We would take the wholesome quality, in this case acceptance and forgiveness, which are the opposite of blame and resentment. We worked on identifying so totally with the virtue that we would not just have it, we would be it. In other words we wouldn't seek so much to forgive as to be forgiveness itself.

In the end resentment and blame leave only when we are forgiveness, rather than when we are trying to forgive. It is a great leap for some, but it is so totally empowering that I recommend trying to be forgiveness until you get. Even if you temporarily fail at it you will have done a lot of forgiving.

An elderly woman said to me after the funeral of her husband, "Most resentments aren't worth a hill of beans in the long run. All the things I blamed him for and resented were a waste of time." Don't wait for someone to die to figure that out. This is a character defect that will die if you don't nourish it. First resentment goes and then even blame. My patient had spent a lot of her life hating some of the things her husband had done. She finally got to the point where she looked at his soul as unblemished spirit. He didn't change. Honestly, all he did was die. She changed. She became forgiveness itself.

Most people are simply too afraid to accept responsibility for themselves. You have to be full of humility to notice the good in others. It takes great faith in human goodness to do that. Instead of having faith in human goodness and being humble, we use the next character flaw, worry, and allow it to expand into fear.

The Dread Seekers—Worry and Fear

HOW DO YOU KNOW IF YOU ARE A *DREAD SEEKER?*

1. Do you feel that you are leading a life of quiet desperation?

2. Do you feel you can never adequately worry about any situation?

3. Do you believe that God is smaller than your problems?

4. Are worry and fear inalienable rights protected by the Constitution?

5. Are you more concerned with things you have no control over?

6. Do you spend time trying to figure out problems that might not occur?

7. Do you dread seek, i.e., worry about what you dread and then try to prove you're right to dread?

8. Do you gloat over how savvy your gloomy predictions of the future are?

9. Are you never too tired to worry?

10. Is worry an effortless process and does it feel natural?

11. Do you spend more time in your imagination with pictures of what you don't want to happen?

12. Do you encourage other people to worry? After all, there can never be too much worrying.

13. Do you argue about what is more important to worry about?

14. Do you get annoyed with people who won't take your worries seriously?

15. Do you live more in the future than the present, and it isn't a good future?

16. Is it easier for you to visualize a negative outcome than a positive one?

17. Do you have constant negative self talk?

18. Do you get immobilized by your fears?

19. Is your nickname Doom and Gloom?

It was Henry David Thoreau who said, "The mass of men lead lives of quiet desperation." Most men aren't leading lives of quiet desperation, regardless of what that famous quote says. In fact most of us complain loudly, bitterly, and frequently about our worries and our fears. There are those of us who do more than complain. Some of us are possessed by this character flaw and become what I call the "dread seekers." These poor souls seek out things in life that they can dread. They are doom-and-gloom forecasters who are stuck in fear. Worry is their dominating state of mind. No amount of reassurance can get them to let go of their vision of how things will be.

It is always the worst possible scenario. With a bold and vivid imagination they embrace the dreaded outcome. Filled with fear and trep-
idation they are dragged kicking and screaming across the finish line
of life.

Dread seekers believe in Murphy's law—that anything that can
go wrong will go wrong—far more than they believe in God. They
hate to be around optimists and seek out careers where it is useful
to predict disaster. You meet them everywhere. The optimist pro-
claims that we live in the best of all possible worlds; and the dread
seeker fears this is true.

Dread seekers are not at peace until they have adequately worried about everything imaginable. And then they have to worry a little
more just to be safe. It is normal, even mature to think things
through and be prepared for a negative consequence. However, when
a person is stuck in fear, and worry domi-
nates his life, he has this character flaw. It
occurs when we try to control things we
have no control over, and imagine outcomes that we dread. When it is like an
addiction and becomes uncontrollable, you

> **Cheer up! The worst is yet
> to come!**
> **—PHILANDER JOHNSON**

have become a dread seeker. Worry and fear have taken over your
mind. Your imagination forebodes constant disaster or failure.

When I was in medical school I had a classmate who spent more
time worrying about exams than studying for them. I used to walk
away from him to keep from having a panic attack out of sympathy.
Nervous Nick, as we called this wiry little guy, could rev anyone up
to a state of frenzy. I loved to annoy Nervous Nick by telling him
how much I enjoyed taking exams.

Dread seekers aren't fun to be around. In fact they are so difficult
to live with that they are almost never portrayed in leading roles in
dramas. Their character just isn't likable enough. They are the stuff
of comedy, however, like Felix Unger in *The Odd Couple* or Don
Knotts in *The Andy Griffith Show*. One of my favorite old-time cartoon characters, Mr. Magoo, is the perfect example of someone who

never worries. That's not because he is so enlightened and unattached from things but because he is so blind that he can't see that he is supposed to worry!

Worry Works!

I heard that Walter Chrysler, the founder of Chrysler Motor Company, used to put everything he was worrying about into a box on his desk. He would wait until the next week to review it. He generally found that most of what he was going to worry about would resolve itself without his worrying. I thought that was a bit Pollyannaish but suggested one of my patients try it. The patient, Harry, was a classical chronic worrier. He immediately wanted to know what kind of box to use. He also wanted to know if he would jinx it if he peeked at the worries during the week. I told him it would. I also told him that whenever he thought about worrying about his problems, to remember that I was thinking about them for him. He made an enormous list of things that he had to worry about. Key phrase here was "had to."

> Don't tell me that worry doesn't do any good. I know better. The things I worry about don't happen.
> —ANONYMOUS

We opened the box the next week. It was filled with some of the most inane and useless things. He was worrying about everything. Almost none of it was under his control. We laughed as he pulled them out. Almost everything he put into the box was already resolved. I still don't know why I haven't used one of those boxes for myself.

A gardener came to see me for depression related to one of his blood pressure medications. It was unusual for him to be depressed. He was one of those fine characters who lived such a clean life that he never worried about anything. He told me that the way he did it was to realize what a waste of emotional energy worry was. He hated to waste energy. He needed it for his gardening. So he quit worrying.

Worry is truly a waste of emotional energy. It turns you into an

Elmer Fudd. Only too late do you realize that most of what you feared was a complete waste of time. For some of us, though, worry and fear are a lifestyle. Creating dread is so automatic that it is constant. Every day we wake up and start worrying. I recognized that there really aren't too many things that you can be certain about in life. The rest you probably should be concerned about, but only if you have some control over them. Otherwise it is a waste of time to worry. You can be certain about death and taxes. That's about it. I'll bet you worry about both of them too, trying to control them.

I have my standard question for people who are dread seekers, these frantic fearful worriers who love to predict doom and gloom. I check to see if they believe in God. If they do, then I ask them how big their God is. I learned a long time ago from some patients in recovery that the most important task for a worrier is to make them compare the size of their God to the size of their problems.

If they have an itty-bitty God and great big problems, we definitely have a dread seeker. I was at a Cocaine Anonymous meeting to celebrate the first year of sobriety for one of my patients. John had lost almost everything through his abuse of cocaine. He had many problems with the IRS. When he finished his story of the trauma he had been through he said, "I believe in a God who is bigger than the IRS. In fact He's bigger than the federal deficit."

How Did It Get Started?

Everyone has something to worry about. I know that's true. You have problems facing you that are great causes for concern. I don't suggest you stop worrying completely. Becoming Mr. Magoo isn't the solution. Even nice people worry. What I am concerned about is worry without taking responsibility to change things. Worry and fear are not inalienable rights. They are patterns of deception played out in the mind as a misguided attempt to cope with life.

Being concerned with things that you can change or can respond to is perfectly normal. It is useful as long as fear and worry produce energy and stimulate you to action. That is not the case with the dread seeker. Paralyzed by his agitated mind, he nonetheless feels he is using his God-given talents.

Agitate, Cogitate, and Vegetate

We were in a group therapy session one evening and a patient, Mary, was rambling on about what she was going to do. She was afraid her next boyfriend would ask her to marry her. Actually it was worse than I make it sound. She hadn't yet finished breaking up with her then boyfriend. We let her ramble on about how bad her marriage was going to be to this next guy. When she was finished, one of the other patients in the group, who hadn't been paying attention, asked, "Mary, when did you get married? Did I miss something?"

Mary said, "He hasn't asked me yet."

Another patient who had become annoyed with the constant worry that this woman brought to the group, said, "Mary, tell her your new boyfriend's name."

"I haven't met him yet," she said.

It provided a bit of comic relief for the group. For my patient, however, the "real fantasy" about meeting and falling in love with another abusive man was a certainty. It took her months to interrupt the dread-seeking pattern. Hopefully you'll see where you do it in your life and put an end to it soon.

It is a common pattern: agitate yourself with worry, then cogitate, or think about it till the worry becomes fear. Finally you are paralyzed by dread.

Robert Frost said, "The reason worry kills more people than work is that more people worry than work." It is difficult to be productive at work while afraid. This is especially true when the fears are groundless. I can shoot at a tiger that I can see, but I can't shoot one that I can't see. The fears I imagine are often far greater than the reality I have to cope with.

Just about anything can stimulate worry. The capacity to worry is linked to our fear of annihilation. By nature we need to be afraid of life-threatening danger. That's why we have the fight-or-flight mechanism programmed into our biology. We have hardwiring that allows us to flee danger automatically. The mechanism revs us up automatically when danger is perceived. It's just that some of us don't turn it off. Since nature has made it harder to relax than to be upset, it is easier to learn to worry than it is to trust. It is certainly easier to fear, or dread, than it is to have faith and hope.

Terror and Timidity

Fear can turn to abject terror relatively quickly, if people feel they will not be able to survive or cope with the things they fear. We each have a mechanism hardwired into our brains for this. If this mechanism triggers spontaneously, then we have a panic attack. Panic attacks are not the same as extreme worry and fear. A person may be gripped by worry and fear and use them with reckless abandon to deal with life's minor difficulties. A panic attack comes out of the blue. It is a biological response, without the stressor. When these attacks are triggered by thinking, there is a therapy called cognitive therapy that works best. Put simply, it means that you change your thinking. When the attacks are truly spontaneous, in my opinion, medications are most effective.

The difference between a chronic worrier and a person with panic is interesting. The chronic worrier will more often be moody, the doom-and-gloom type, and not be clinically depressed. The patient with panic disorder is more likely not to be moody and pessimistic but will periodically be clinically depressed. This stuff is not written in stone. If you think you have major depression or panic disorder, get a referral to a professional. A bus driver who suffered from panic disorder put it this way. The process from worry to fear to panic may take the same route, but each is a different sort of vehicle.

You know if you are a worrier. Do you love your own gloomy predictions about the future? If you do, then you're a worrier. You agree with Thoreau and say, "Nothing is so much to be feared as fear."

Terror induced by this character flaw serves to create timidity, not a stimulus to action. These fears are projections of our own underlying problems. They are not based on reality. Dread seekers need to create scenarios that are larger than life. The scenarios are as grandiose as the dread seekers' fantasies. That way these people can settle back and choose to do nothing, because their fears are bigger than they are. Their fears are remnants of the past where they couldn't cope, patched into the fabric of their future.

You Don't Have to Try to Worry?

Okay, let's suppose you are one of those people who worries in an effortless manner. You are probably not glad that this stuff comes so easily to you. You would prefer to be fearless. All dread seekers make that claim. Worry and fear start by themselves, even without our permission. Fearlessness is an illusion. When we don't have fear that is appropriate we are either counterphobic or leaving ourselves sitting ducks for disaster.

A counterphobe is a person who has the opposite of panic attacks. This is the person who sees danger and feels fear, then decides that he or she must face it. Often it is just for the sake of one's own entertainment. This person will bungee jump, skydive, and do a whole host of dangerous things. What he or she is really trying to do is master this character flaw through action. When you get to the point where you no longer have complete freedom of choice and must take every risk in order to overcome your fears, then the character flaw has turned you into a counterphobe.

Never Too Tired to Worry!

Are you never too tired to worry either? Worry is a common response to being hungry, angry, lonely, or tired. HALT. Worry is a just a normal safeguard when you are emotionally depleted. If you find yourself worrying for no apparent reason, stop. Take a look at whether you are hungry, angry, lonely, or tired.

There is a primitive part of the brain that signals you to worry when hunger goes a little too far, or you have been away from others and are isolated. We are social beings and need to be with others. Worrying when you are alone will enhance survival.

I Worry Therefore I Am!

The problem with the dread seeker is that he worries in any situation. The criteria is, still breathing and still thinking, therefore still worrying. Or as Descartes might have written, "I worry, therefore I am." There is a famous threefold expression of who you are in Sanskrit. It is Chith, Sath, and Annanda, or being, awareness, and bliss. For the dread seeker it is essence, worry, and fear. This is their experience of reality.

Regardless of what colors our worry, it always comes back to obsessively using the mind to create pictures of things we don't wish to occur. The process is the same.

Worry Makes Our Moral Dilemmas Visible

I think it may have been Elbert Hubbard who said, "The thing we fear we bring to pass." It is in most major scriptures too. Job said, "What I fear overtakes me." Worry is a way for us to handle our moral dilemmas. When we are unsure, conflicted, tentative, or uncertain, worry feels like a solution.

I have a friend who is a screenwriter. He used to say that conflict is what salvages the middle of every movie. If moral dilemma isn't portrayed, then the character is dull and boring. That's why we like to watch the crises that occur in others. Dread seekers are often trying to avoid being bored. At the same time they want to put their own life's problems aside rather than confront them. The worries they have reflect issues that need work, but the character flaw causes the paralysis that keeps them from acting on it. That is why this character flaw is so crippling.

Numerous patients have come to me to talk about their fears of being cheated on by their partner. It is a major issue for people who themselves have the desire to be unfaithful. As they try to suppress the desire within themselves, the fear of infidelity by their partner surfaces to replace it. Patients fall apart over the fantasy of an affair that their partner hasn't had. This is done under the pretext that if they could cope with it in their fantasies, then they would be able to cope with it in reality. It's too bad that this never works. The trauma is greater when it happens in reality. All their worries don't help at all.

It works the same way for suffering too. Usually the person who fears suffering is already suffering from what he fears. His worries have given way to a more genuine and intense experience. Let me illustrate this for you. An elderly man came to my office to complain that he was going blind and couldn't deal with it. He was grieving the loss of his eyesight a few years before he was going to go blind. His misery was so acute that I almost hospitalized him. He was distraught about something real but in the future. He had brought all the pain, agony, and darkness of his future into the present and was unable to deal with it.

The Ripple Effect—Fear Flunkies!

If you have ever been with a group of fearful people working themselves up, then you know what happens. One person has a concern. Another person expresses a belief that the concern is valid. A third will join in and let them both know that they can never worry too much about that one!

On and on it goes. They build into a frenzy using other people as their fear flunkies. They are partners in panic trying to make sure that they are adequately afraid. They are more than just pessimists. They are dread seekers. They are nourished by a belief that hope sets you up for disappointment and faith gets you sucker punched by life. They love to watch other people worry like they do.

Worrying for Someone Else Is Easier!

Try worrying for someone else. The first time a friend of mine did this to me I thought he was kidding. I was in a prayer group and one of the guys said, "Hey, T, now that we prayed for it, do you think you could stop worrying about it?"

"I don't know," I said laughing at him.

"I'm serious," he said. "The next time you start to worry about it, just remind yourself that the rest of us believe that it will be okay. In fact whenever you start to doubt, worry, or fear, know that we believe for you even if you can't."

Sure I was shocked. I'm a doctor. I get paid to worry. I'm a psychiatrist so I could worry about anything I wanted and justify it. My friend took away my right to worry. Not only that, he replaced it with a belief that my prayer was answered even when I doubted. Follow me on that. It's not really that confusing. Whenever I doubted, I could remind myself that the other people in my group didn't doubt. They were believing for me.

I started doing that with my patients. It was especially useful between the time a person started treatment and recovered. I let my patients know that I believed they would get better. Anytime they worried about that, they should remind themselves that I believed they would recover. This is how a couple can support each other when one is going through something. Try it next time someone you love is worried. If such a person is addicted to fear and worry he or she will get indignant with you. Otherwise he or she will be grateful.

Worried Wives and Harried Husbands

Often spouses drag their partners into my office complaining bitterly that they didn't worry about the same things. Thank God, or they would have driven each other crazy and been divorced already. New-lyweds frequently run into this problem. One is a bigger worrier than the other. They argue about how much concern is being shown. They fight over how empathic and sympathetic they are.

It takes years to learn how to worry equally about the same things. Mothers worry differently about children than fathers. Wives worry differently than husbands. Men worry differently about money than women. At least men believe that.

A Generation of Worried Children!

The baby boomers were a generation raised on shared worries. It was pointed out to us that we needed to worry about all sorts of things. For instance as a child I had to worry about fitting under my desk and covering my head completely with my arms as the thermonuclear device blew up over Morristown, New Jersey. It was explained in great detail that the bombs would be aimed at New York, miss, and hit Morristown. I secretly hoped I would have enough time. I didn't want to hit my head on the desk and I was afraid I would burn my arms. So we practiced.

Every generation is raised on shared concerns. My little ones are afraid of ozone depletion, rain forest destruction, and global warming. I make sure that I tell them about global warming on the coldest day I can find in February. I hate to talk about it in the summer. That wouldn't do much for their fears.

We create fears in each new generation and hope that these fears help to motivate our children to live right. They learn a lot about what to fear from parents and from their peers.

Doom and Gloom

I can't resist telling you about my father's hard hat. Dad was one of those guys beloved by half the people who knew him and loathed by the other half. He was a funeral director. More than that Dad was a convinced pessimist. He loved Murphy's law. That was the only book I ever saw him read; usually he just read obituaries. During my medical school years I spent a couple of summers working construction as a carpenter. My dad was involved in the project. Whenever he visited the site, he wore a hard hat. On the front was written "D&G."

"What's the 'D&G'?" I asked.

"Doom and gloom," said one of the workers. "Your father worries about everything. He is certain that every part of the project will go wrong. He worries enough for all the rest of us."

I should do a movie script about him. I could call it *Night of the Living Gloom*. Personally, I reacted to his doom and gloom by becoming an undying optimist.

Little boys need examples to live by. They have to model behaviors that will help them survive. The walking gloomy don't help children survive. Kids need positive examples. It is imperative that we make examples of people who have healthy attitudes, great character, and have overcome adversity. Children have an innate ability to seek out positive influences.

All sorts of fears surface when people have children. Often their natural concern becomes a character flaw when there has been an illness in the child. Sometimes it happens when the child is ready to go off to college or get married. We have to vent our concerns for our children through caring. It makes us feel useful. The empty-nest syndrome usually occurs in the parent who did the most worrying. That is normally the mother, but not always. It embarrassed men to tell me about their mixed-up feelings when their children moved away. It was supposed to be just the women who felt this way.

On the Sunny Side of the Flaw

There must be a good intention behind dread seeking.

Dread seeking can teach you where you might have an addicted belief. An addicted belief is a belief that you maintain even though you keep getting bad results from it. You are addicted to keeping the belief in spite of the pain it causes. The flaw is trying to motivate you to action. That's why you worry. It's just that too much fear immobilizes.

Worry and fear help us recognize our true values or criteria. We worry about what is most important to us. If you worry more about your work than your family, you have placed an enormous amount of value on work. I don't tell you that to make you feel guilty, though this flaw may help you discover some areas of guilt. It is not necessarily bad to feel guilty. If it helps you develop better character and make the world a better place, then I am all for it.

Fear and worry may be the only signals you get that you are in danger. We unconsciously overstep our bounds with all sorts of people. Sometimes fear is a signal to take a look at the boundaries. I can remember telling the chairman of a surgery department what I thought of his attitude. Later I worried. I had to take a look at the boundaries between chairmen and resident physicians.

Worry guards against real or imagined danger. The larger the imagined danger, the larger the worry and the greater the need is for action. Fear and worry may serve as a shield from harm. Trust that if you don't obsessively worry, a little fear might be an alarm.

I have never met a master in any sport who didn't try to run through his performance in his mind's eye. The greats come up with solutions to the worst possible scenario. They are not immobilized by it. In a sense that ensures peace. Being peaceful often is associated with peak performance.

Fear and worry can help you socially. It could help you respond to the opinion of others. When you obsess about the opinion of others, it's the character flaw in action, not normal worry.

I have stated it before, fear and worry are part of your survival mechanism. They are also clues to understanding deeper needs. Where fear is, a need may be hiding. Normal worry can be used as a signal to empower you to take action, whereas dread and obsessive worry shut you down. Your needs aren't taken care of but in fact cause you to neglect your needs with an emotional paralysis.

Courage, not Fearlessness: How to Worry Properly

Courage is action in spite of your fears. It is being afraid but holding on just a little longer. "Hang in there, baby," reads the poster with a cat hanging from a branch. You may be on the verge of creating vast self-knowledge by facing your fears and controlling how you worry. Looking at any character flaw can be enlightening, but this one helps you understand how you prepare yourself for life. Worry is preparation in the arena of the mind. If you are not prepared to face the things you fear, then you have not been worrying properly.

You are already aware of the fact that your self talk influences how you feel when you worry. In group therapy we would take a person's big worry and have them say it out loud in the same tone that they used for their self talk. Usually people don't like to share the tone they use in their head when they worry. It's embarrassing. Then we would take suggestions from the group on how to talk to yourself. It was fun to see how the worries changed.

You also know that your visualizations can affect the intensity of your fears. In group we would encourage smaller and fuzzier pictures of the things feared. You have the power to control this. It will enable you to channel the power of worry into more effective deterrents and defenses. You can't ensure that things will turn out the way you want them to, but you can worry less.

How do you worry less? Worry only about the parts of a situation over which you have direct control. If you are going to fantasize about possible outcomes, don't just conjure up the worst one. Consider some probable, less negative, or even positive outcomes, too.

You can fend off an unwanted attack if you are prepared. Then worry becomes an assurance that you have taken the necessary precautions. Dread seekers are secretly searching for ways to feel in control when it is unrealistic to do so. Give up trying to control what you can't.

Let worry remind you to think about results, or outcomes, not problems. We make assessments in medicine in order to formulate a plan, not to sit and reminisce with patients about the days when they were healthy. If a doctor came in, sat down, and said, "You're ill. You have chest pain. We call it angina. You should worry that you don't feel well. Now let's think about a time in your past when you felt better," you'd throw him right out!

Understand FEAR for What It Is

I love to collect these little acronyms for big ideas. We had hundreds of them in medical school. When I got into residency training I was handed a book of abbreviations from the Health and Hospital Corporation. Most of them were acronyms. Often acronyms can help you understand a common idea.

WORRY: Wonderful Outcomes Really Release You.

Now take FEAR. Most commonly this is an acronym for False Expectations Appearing Real. If you take a good look at the character flaw based on what I have written, you will see that it is Fantasized Experiences Attacking Relentlessly.

But suppose FEAR really was Future Enjoyment Avoiding Reality. How would that change your attitude toward your fears? Would you be willing to face your fears? Emerson said, "Do the thing you fear and the death of fear is certain." When you understand what fear really is you find that it is even more than your future enjoyment. Those who face fears come out exalted, empowered, richer for having faced the thing they feared. FEAR turned out to be Future Empowerment/Exaltation Awaiting Revelation.

The only sane thing to do is to face the thing you fear. Sanity is having the integrity to face your fears. Here's how.

WHEN LIFE REALLY GETS INSANE!

- Get back into the NOW
- Give yourself a reality check
- Visualize your positive outcome
- Hang on to integrity
- Most likely scenario: Honesty
- Use positive self talk
- Accept results-oriented emotions—do a flux
- Change what you can, surrender the rest

The very first step is to get back into the NOW—Notice the Outside World. Stop for a moment and look around you. Often we are so preoccupied with future fantasies and the insane ramblings of our vivid imaginations that we forget to notice where we are. Stay focused on the here and now. It will bring you back to reality. It is harder to maintain fear of a dreaded future if you can stay in the now moment.

Give yourself a reality check. I suggest that you give yourself a worst-case scenario. Go ahead and embellish it all you want. What is the worst that could possibly happen? Make it as bad as you would like. Then reality-test it. How likely is it? Have you realistically looked at all the data?

Now ask yourself what is the most likely outcome, not just the worst possible outcome. Which is really more important? The one that is most likely going to happen or that which you fear the most?

I know you want more control or you wouldn't be worrying. So visualize your desired outcome. Since you are going to fantasize, fantasize what you would like to have happen. It is important to have some idea of what you want. Look to see if you actually want something you have any control over. It is interesting to watch worriers' fantasies. They think about things they can't control. That helps them worry better. I have dealt with some real expert worriers in my day. They surrender their personal integrity just to be right.

Facing a situation that stimulates feelings of dread can be harder than you think. It will always be easier if you are honest. Sometimes that requires a strong determination to turn off your pictures of the future and get back into the now for a few moments. Fear doesn't let you do that easily.

You must also practice positive self talk. Let me explain what I mean. You probably have an image of the salesman at a rally saying yes I can! I can do it! I will do it! That's not what I am talking about.

Positive self talk is telling yourself whatever you need to hear to be able to function while maintaining personal integrity. It is speaking honestly to yourself about the future. For most of us, that means toning down our dreaded outcomes and being more realistic. It is talking about going on, in spite of the negative feelings you may have, because going on is the right thing to do.

> **Let us be of good cheer, remembering that the misfortunes hardest to bear are those which never happen.**
> **—JAMES RUSSELL LOWELL**

Positive self talk also means accepting what I call results-oriented emotions. Here is an example. A patient came in devastated after a major failure at work. She was angry for a while, then frustrated. The frustration shifted to determination and finally back to motivation. We shift like this all the time. You determine how long it takes to make the shift. Positive self talk encourages you to make these shifts, maintain your integrity, and be committed to courageousness.

I had a patient who always whined to himself and convinced himself that his negative thinking was true and accurate. I teased him because he believed that if it was negative it was more likely to be true. One day he asked me to reprogram his brain. He had listened to positive-thinking tapes and a few motivational speakers but "knew" he couldn't get what they meant. I had him imagine a tape recorder on which he had taped his negative self talk about a current project. It was a low-energy whining affirmation about what losers he and this project were. Then I had him tape a positive enthusiastic message about himself on the same imaginary tape. He wanted to tape over his negative message but his recorder wouldn't allow that. He taped the positive and very accurate self talk after the negative message. Then he played the whole tape repeatedly. He did the first part faster and faster and listened carefully to the last part. After a while every time his head played the negative tape it was fast, jumbled, and followed up by the positive affirmation. The change was remarkable.

There is nothing courageous about getting stuck in fear. You have to face it and change the things you can. You have to move through it. You have to hope even when despair comes easier. Fear must serve as the clarion call for your soul to rally. At some level it is faith and not logic that will overcome fears. Remember that hope is brightest when it dawns from the depths of your fears.

Accept the world on its terms before you try to change it. This will reduce your fears. Not accepting reality will increase them dramatically. It is the basis of another flaw, intolerance.

Intolerance

HOW DO YOU KNOW IF YOU HAVE *INTOLERANCE?*

1. Are you intolerant of people, places, and things?

2. Do you have an attitude of disdain?

3. Have you ever been accused of acting morally superior to others?

4. Do you believe Rodney Dangerfield is correct and "can't get no respect"?

5. Do you have a chip on your shoulder?

6. Are you disinclined to give people the benefit of the doubt?

7. Do you use the word "disgusting" often?

8. Do you believe that most people have little self-control?

9. Are you a skeptic?

10. Do you think people are phony?

11. Are you intolerant of your own flaws but make no effort to change?

12. Are you intolerant of playful children?

13. Do you get offended very easily?

14. Do you secretly believe that when you are intolerant you are still putting your best foot forward?

15. Do you believe some people don't bring any added benefit to relationships?

16. Are you intolerant of how other people look?

17. Do you find some religions, races, or nationalities irritating?

18. Are you annoyed by other people's virtues?

19. Do you lose your patience easily?

"What do you want," the instructor said to me as I walked into her office. "I have enough to do today and there is an epidemic of stupidity out there in which everyone seems to be participating." She stopped talking and blew out air through pursed lips. "You better not have a crisis. My schedule is full."

Have you ever noticed that some people are intolerant of a few essentials, like people, places, things, and ideas? You know the type. They are the die-hard intolerants. These die-hards are the clever elite who will blacklist you in their minds for not fitting into their picture of how the world is supposed to be. Even though you may be a part of their reality you don't belong in it. They are experts in rejection. They disrespect people with whom they disagree.

Can't Get No Respect

Even though you know intolerance is there, you may not be able to define it. It is not as blatant as resentment. It certainly controls itself better than raging indignation. Though it is intimately related to addicted to being right it can camouflage itself as compassion and understanding. The die-hard intolerant acts as though he is wiser than you. It can look like elegance to the upper class. His intolerance will show its face as wisdom to the learned. It will look like strength to the powerful and like passion to the committed.

> **Little things affect little minds.**
> —BENJAMIN DISRAELI

An attitude of superiority and disdain pervades the air when this flaw is present. This attitude of rejection and intolerance is the basis of bias and prejudice. Sometimes it is blatant, like racial prejudice or nationalism. Sometimes it is very subtle and presents itself as pity for the poor unfortunates who aren't as liberated, or enlightened, as we are. Nevertheless, it is still intolerance.

Hey, There's a Chip on Your Shoulder!

We make fun of intolerance and celebrate it with comedy. It is one of the ways that we diffuse the character flaw. It would be easier if we were as open about our intolerance as Bud Abbott was with Lou Costello. Abbott made no bones about it. He believed Lou Costello was inept and needed to be admonished frequently. Instead our intolerance often conceals itself with moral superiority. What does it mean to be intolerant of the behavior of another? It is not just prejudging but is severe rejection of others without justification.

You've heard, "I give everybody the benefit of the doubt." What these masters of repudiation are really saying is they can pretend to have patience before they judge and reject you. They explain how they listened. Then they dump all over you, after you have graciously benefited from their doubt. Like most people they are closed-minded about all sorts of things. It is inevitable that people grow up with some prejudice, but since that is not the way enlightened beings are supposed to act, they pretend that they are understanding. Chances are there was no benefit to you from their doubt. It was a way to ambush you with abuse and rejection.

Watch prime-time TV and you see the whole host of characters who are intolerant. Watch sitcoms to see if people are given the benefit of the doubt or are judged immediately. Intolerance is everywhere. It is like an infectious disease. Of all the character flaws, this one hides behind phony concern and yet readily transmits itself to others. It is like a computer virus that infects every system it comes in contact with. We become intolerant without noticing. It happens automatically.

Contamination of the Soul

Bob and Mary came to my office to work on their relationship. They wanted to heal the rift that had developed between them but couldn't seem to work it out on their own. He was a successful businessman and she was in a middle-management position. They were used to managing other people, yet they couldn't manage the most important relationship in their lives. They couldn't figure out what had gone wrong, so I asked them to think about when it started. Their insight was quite intriguing. They realized that at some point in their relationship they had developed intolerance for a few simple quirks. She liked to leave dishes in the sink at night and that reminded him of his ex-wife. He had to refold the newspaper so it looked unread. She pulled pages out that she was interested in. They realized that they had stopped trusting each other. Trust and intolerance can't live together.

They stopped having fun and started checking to see if what they feared was true. Slowly the intolerance seeped in. Intolerance shifts to blame and resentment and dooms the relationship. It is salvaged only through great doses of forgiveness. Intolerance breeds resentment. It reflects the flaw addicted to being right. Intolerance is like a root system in a forest of character flaws. It keeps them connected and nurturing one another.

The Unreliability Prayer

Intolerance causes you to have distorted thinking. The alcoholic has the Serenity Prayer. Die-hard intolerants have their intolerance prayer. They know with every fiber of their being that people are unreliable and have selfish motives for their behavior. Let me share their secret prayer with you:

> *God grant me the power to be intolerant of the things I do not accept,*
> *The deviousness to control the things I think I need,*
> *And the cunning to see the real motives of others.*

Intolerance is the bridge of insanity that links the other character defects together. You don't have to agree with someone, but you do need to respect their right to believe differently. Normally this flaw causes you to resent others' beliefs. If you resent someone's beliefs you reject them. Whenever you fight over being right, you risk becoming intolerant in other areas of the relationship.

The Calamari Test

If you hear the words "That's disgusting," you're probably listening to someone who is intolerant. As a test, ask someone if they like to eat squid. Half of the people in the USA have never even tried it. Nonetheless, most who are asked will say, "I don't like it. It's not for me." If they've tried it they might tell you, "That's disgusting." They think that by saying it is disgusting they have proved to you that they were right. If they haven't tried squid, have them try calamari. Most of the time they will tell you that it is interesting, delicious, or that they didn't like the flavor. Because you gave it an exotic foreign name they become a little more tolerant.

Nasty Animals

When I was in medical school I used to raise parrots. I got pretty comfortable handling very large birds. One day a veterinarian who was a friend asked me if I would help him with a large and nasty macaw. I was young and didn't have an adequately developed sense of fear. So I went over to the pet shop. I walked into this large cage with gloves on to hold the bird for my friend. I should have started psychotherapy that day, because I needed my head examined. The bird was friendly as could be. It barely reacted to me when I entered. It let me touch it, pet it, and do just about anything I wanted. I almost took my leather gloves off because it was so friendly.

What I didn't know was that the bird only had so much tolerance for human contact. It was unpredictable. I couldn't read its level of intolerance and got suckered in. I went from holding this beautiful creature for the vet to having the creature hold me. My thumb was crushed in the strongest beak I had ever experienced.

You probably have some birds like that where you work too. They hide their intolerance until it is time to attack.

Or maybe you work around snarling dogs? They are actually quite safe. They let you know that they are getting intolerant. They are easier to deal with.

Education Without Wisdom

We spend billions each year on education. We teach facts. We cram little heads full of information. By the time a child is in third grade he or she either knows more information about the world than was known by the average university graduate a hundred years ago or can't read. We teach courses that are supposed to help kids become more tolerant, yet look around you and you will see most of them aren't. We have a society that caters to rampant egoism. There are so many people trying to get into the limelight, looking for that moment of fame. We worship information as though it was some sort of god who could liberate us from bondage. We don't teach children how to think for themselves, to be wise. We don't teach timeless values or virtues like respect and righteousness; instead we teach sex education. Instead of honor and duty we teach rights. We educate by information, not by teaching wisdom.

Education without wisdom is fertile ground for intolerance. Given a little bit of rationalization we can justify any belief we want. When your beliefs don't match mine, I become intolerant. If I am lazy or insecure in my thinking, I reject your thoughts. Watch any child confront something that is different, like a bug or a worm. Children who are insecure will become afraid. They can't tolerate it. If they are secure they will become curious. The worm becomes a thing of beauty and joy.

As we get older our intolerance becomes more stubborn. We become die-hard intolerants. The character defect becomes extremely durable. We then learn that we must hide it at times and only let it surface when we are around other like-minded individuals. There we can nurture it, perfect it.

If intolerance is so bad, why am I so good at it?

WHAT DOES IT REVEAL?

- A prior trauma and an honest desire to protect oneself
- A fear of loss or loss of control
- A misperception of others' motives
- A belief that you belong to a special group
- A need to share your morality
- An inability to see things from someone else's view
- A lack of functional boundaries
- A lack of emotional toughness

You are good at intolerance because **you had a prior trauma** and now you need to protect yourself from repeating it. A trauma may have occurred so early on in your life that you don't even know which event caused it. It is there ready to motivate you at every turn. Almost everyone has been burned at some point in his or her life. It may have been child abuse or a judgmental parent. It might have been a teacher or a coach.

This flaw surfaces automatically when **you fear a loss**. I've watched patients who were told that they needed surgery get intolerant with their doctors. The fear of the loss, either of life or limb, stimulates intolerance. In other patients there is a sense of gratitude because they thought they were going to die; instead they are getting a lifesaving surgery. Both patients may have the same disease. One has the flaw while the other has gratitude.

Sometimes the **fear is of the loss of control**. Watch people who get irritable before a situation that requires trust. Intolerance colors everything they do, even when they know it won't help. Intolerant people become annoyed more easily than others. A friend of mine missed his flight and became intolerant almost to the point of raging indignation. He sat and watched the plane taxi out and get stuck on the runway with a mechanical failure. When they finally got the plane back, he was one of the lucky ones who was already seated on the next flight. He had become intolerant with the check-in people because he felt he was going to lose the opportunity to get home on time. In fact he got home earlier than if he had gotten on the first plane.

I have already mentioned that intolerance presupposes the **worst possible motives** for someone else's behavior. How often have you been asked, "What do you want?" accompanied by a huff or blowing out of air. Huffing is a signal to you that the other person knows your motive is bad. He is ready for you. Sometimes a very controlled person will hide it, but most of the time we forget to monitor our breathing and it gives us away.

The "chosen people syndrome" occurs when you believe you are justified in being intolerant to others, usually a group, because you are part of another **special group**. The group is somehow chosen by God. We all need to belong. Intolerance is a wacky way for people to show membership in the group of the chosen. Some of my colleagues at the university were intolerant of the physicians who were in private practice because they weren't part of the intellectually superior group. Hopefully they worked on this in their therapy.

This chosen-group phenomenon starts very early. Watch a group of third graders pick on the second graders. Watch one ethnic group demean another. Being part of a special group helps us survive. We band together for strength and support. We feed off the "group esteem" to bolster our low self-esteem. Often the group esteem feeds on putting down other groups. Being intolerant of others never makes us stronger. Vigilance with open-mindedness does. Being intolerant of others is a sign of low self-esteem. It is the working of an insecure ego trying to deal with others by rejecting them.

Groups of the "specially chosen" are **trying to teach a shared morality**. That in and of itself is good. The problem with teaching shared morality is that intolerant people don't want to teach it by example, they want to beat it into you. They focus their attention on showing you how to reject people who don't have your morality. They may hide it by telling you to pray for them, but you know when it is intolerance. This character flaw is clever, isn't it?

Many people are extremely intolerant of anything they can't understand because of their inability to shift perspectives and **see things from someone else's view**. They are so allergic to reality that coping with their own perspective is stress enough. I often asked my clients to try and see it from the other person's view. You would think that I were asking them to drink poison.

We have that old issue of **functional boundaries**, too. Rather than develop boundaries from a sense of self and wholeness, intolerant people have shifting boundaries designed to protect their very sensitive egos. On one day you can joke with them. On another day your humor is grating on their nerves. Their boundaries have shifted.

Worse yet the intolerant cunningly set up different sets of boundaries for different people. The more secure and mature a person is, the more likely it is that his or her boundaries will be stable from day to day and from group to group. If you are wondering why the artfully intolerant shift their boundaries so often, it's simple. They either need to manipulate you or they are trying to control their own out-of-whack feelings.

> If we had to tolerate in others all that we permit in ourselves, life would become completely unbearable.
> —GEORGES COURTLIN

Intolerance pretends to be a sign of great strength in our society. Watch the famous sports stars who get annoyed with little children asking for autographs. It is actually a sign of a lack of emotional toughness. Where you find someone practicing the art of intolerance, being deliberately rude to protect his or her poor, overinflated ego, you will find someone who is afraid, weak, and insecure. What is used as the symbol of strength is nothing more than a mask for inadequacy. Watch the celebrities **who project an image of intolerance as part of** their promotion. When it is no longer an act but is automatic you are seeing someone with deep problems.

The Demise of Delight!

Sadly those who are under the sway of intolerance suffer a life of great loss. Because this flaw has become such an ingrained pattern they don't have the slightest notion of what it is that they are missing. They have lost their ability to marvel at life. They no longer have that childlike capacity for fascination. Things they don't understand are rejected. Let's take a quick look at the damage intolerance does to:

- Delight
- Ideas

- Relationships
- Inner strength
- Self-knowledge

Intolerance is not just the opposite of tolerance. It is the opposite of something far greater: delight. We have this amazing capacity to view life in a poetic sense. We see meaning rather than just facts. We have the potential to experience the bliss of being alive in every moment of existence. Most of us never view the sunrise; we are intolerant of waking early. Most of us don't stop and smell the flowers; our automobiles are moving too fast. This allergy to reality is so pervasive that it takes what could be delightful and turns it into something to be wary of.

We lose our capacity to relish ideas other than our own. If you don't agree with what I am already thinking, I become annoyed, jealous, or envious. The delight vanishes and the idea is missed. Sometimes crucial ideas are missed and we suffer needlessly. We go back later and the second time we hear the idea along with, "I tried to tell you before, but you wouldn't even listen."

We abandon our new relationships before they have a chance to form. These relationships could deepen our humanity and expand our horizons. Yet we do not delight in them but rather create a wall of intolerance. If the person has the ability to scale our defenses and survive our tests, then we risk opening up. We ask others to take the chip off our shoulder before they can become our friend.

When I first started treating addicts and alcoholics, I "missed" a lot of patients because they were intolerant of physicians. They had experienced a subtle form of abuse at the hands of other doctors. These "other doctors" were "enablers" who didn't know much about recovery. In fact, through good intentions they had managed to make the disease worse.

Later I learned to take the chip off the patient's shoulder by sharing my story of recovery. I learned that from the counselors who worked with me and from my colleagues who are physicians in recovery. They delighted in removing the chip. Slipping around the wall of intolerance was part of the art of good therapy. With every type of illness getting around the wall was fun. It was an art. It was delightful.

If you have missed the delightful poetry of human relationships because you are intolerant, then you probably have missed drinking at the inner wellspring of

> **Bigotry dwarfs the soul by shutting out the truth.**
> **—EDWIN HUBBEL CHAPIN**

creativity that nourishes your hidden strengths. When someone challenges our old beliefs an outpouring of new resources can suddenly fill our being. It is like watching a personal transformation with time-lapse photography. It is rapid and dramatic.

We had a young lady in group who had been abused by a series of men. The experience culminated in a tragic suicide attempt. She had focused all her intolerance on herself. I call that self-rejection. The consequence was more subtle than the suicide attempt. This was a woman who had never risen to her potential. She was bright, articulate, yet unable to achieve. At some point she let go of the flaw. She didn't just practice tolerance with herself but marveled at this creation by God that she called her "self." I can pinpoint the day she made the breakthrough in group. So can the other counselors, because she got younger. So much stress was released that people started to wonder if she'd had a face lift.

Marveling became her new inner strength. It enabled her to discover things about herself that had been hidden from her for years. She used to resent people telling her that she could do more, be more, and have more. Now she knew she was far more than she had previously realized. Letting go of intolerance opened her up to greater self-knowledge.

Giving Your Power Away

One day a furniture salesman came into my office. He checked out the chairs before he sat down. This was a man who had always been able to take care of his family. Suddenly a series of business problems caused him to lose the family store. "I am a tightwad, Doc. I count pennies and I am terrified that we will lose everything."

His wife had taken over part of the responsibility for the family's financial support. She had chosen to spend a number of years away from work, raising her children. Now that her children were adults she had gone back to work with renewed passion. In response, he had became intolerant and verbally abusive. He suffered from the shame of losing his earning power, and had to deal with his petty jealousy.

After a short time in therapy he began to realize that whenever he was intolerant he was giving his power away by allowing other people to control his emotions. He decided to economize. That was the only hook I had to get him to look at what was going on. He managed to cut off the intolerance and deal with the loss of the business, the grief, and the inadequacy.

At about the same time I had a middle-aged man come in who told me the story of his marriage to a very successful woman. They had been high school sweethearts. He needed to do physical work, so he chose outside construction, while she pursued an MBA. They had a stormy time the first few years after her graduation. "I know she is the smarter one in the relationship," he said to me. "It was difficult to face at first, but then it dawned on me that we were partners. Being smarter than your wife was not a requirement for being a good husband or good father."

Sometimes being tolerant of our own relative weakness in a relationship will enable us to keep our strength. This is especially true in relationships like marriage, where strengths need to be shared, not given up.

How Does It Affect Your Children?

If you're a parent, then like the rest of us you probably have one of the most beautiful children in the world. If you don't believe that, your child is probably now a teenager. You better learn how to marvel.

Children often develop the same type of intolerance that we have. We develop a blind eye to their character flaws. Even the most beautiful apple can have a worm in it. You need to be intolerant of wrong behavior, but you can't parent from intolerance. We are sometimes intolerant of silly things like our children making noise at a religious service. God, they're kids. They eat, cry, and soil themselves.

It takes more tolerance some days than others to parent. I find it especially true when my children try to get away with all the stuff I got away with. Tolerance reflects love. Intolerance of immorality is essential and reflects love too. One of the good uses of intolerance is to shut down disrespect as soon as it occurs. This is difficult for children. We have to teach it continuously. Children naturally want to feel free. They use disrespect to delude themselves into believing that they are free.

> **Human diversity makes tolerance more than a virtue; it makes it a requirement of survival.**
> —RENÉ DUBOS

Surviving the Wake of Intolerance

Think about that quote above. Tolerance is more than a virtue. It is a requirement for survival. Tolerance is one of the first things to go when someone is emotionally ill. I had a patient who became more intolerant when he was going into a manic episode. His family would watch his sales performance and could determine how he was doing. That is undoubtedly unusual. Most of the time when people get sick their illness catches everybody off guard.

In business most clients are not lost to competition due to a better product. Most clients are not lost to competition due to pricing. Most of the time clients are lost because of intolerance on the part of someone working at the business. I have a friend whose phone staff were impolite and intolerant of his clients. The situation was so bad that he had to fire a number of people. His gross income doubled over the next year with the help of friendlier staff. That pattern is obvious to anyone who has ever been in management.

Inoculation Against Intolerance?

Watch the gentlemen at the fast-food counter next time you are being served. There is always at least one who is practicing intolerance. He'll be standing there, with a chip on his shoulder, ready to take your order. What is actually going on is that he is ready to attack you. He has temporarily lulled himself into believing he is on his best behavior by being intolerant. That's because he thinks die-hard intolerance is a better choice than his alternative, rage. Once you understand when you are not on your best behavior by being intolerant, you will be on the road to understanding a lot about the other flaws that haunt you.

> **Nothing dies so hard, or rallies so often, as intolerance.**
> **—HENRY WARD BEECHER**

Die-hard Intolerance

Intolerance demands that we learn to trust God and be honest about people. We pretend that our intolerance somehow shows that we have discovered a flaw in someone else. The truth is just the opposite. Often it signals our weakness, and displays our inadequacies.

Die-hard intolerance is related to self-rejection. As I have stated before, self-esteem is at issue when you are intolerant. People who are real die-hards have become intolerant of their own negative feelings too. People with low self-esteem make the mistake of believing that if they have a painful feeling, then the feeling is bad. That's not true at all. The feelings are painful simply because that is how they feel. We need to recognize all our emotions as simply what they are, feelings. It's okay to have all sorts of feelings. By the way, if anyone tells you that you are what you feel, shake them for me. That is one of those ridiculous ideas that has been around forever. Yet it continues to perpetuate itself. You are the experiencer or observer of your feelings, not the feelings themselves. You aren't negative or bad because you have "negative" feelings.

Dance to the Beat of a Different Drummer

So what is the key to unlocking intolerance's secrets? How do you take a moment of intolerance and transform it into a lesson that becomes a blessing, a healing, and reveals a hidden gain? What virtues do you have to practice to counteract the flaw? How is life different when you are no longer automatically intolerant? In order to do that you will have to dance, not march to the beat of a different drummer. Here are the essential dance steps.

- Every person brings a lesson
- Every event is a blessing
- Every heartache is a healing
- Every loss is a hidden gain
- Patience is the only virtue you will ever need
- Life is marvelous

Every person brings a lesson. View every person that you encounter as a teacher of some lesson in life. When I was a medical student there was a little baby who was born with a large portion of his intestines missing. One of the nurses in the neonatal ICU developed a particularly strong attachment to the child. She cared for him for months. She explained to me that the child had taught many young interns and residents how to be better doctors. At one point a new resident even wrote an order to teach the baby to say "mama." It was wonderful to watch the nurses carry the order out. It was even more wonderful to see the look in the eyes of the baby's mother.

They could have let the child just be a case. They decided to learn how to be more caring and loving. It is easier with children than it is with adults. Some of the lessons that adults bring us are extremely difficult to tolerate. They teach us to be more loving. Sometimes they show us where we are hypocrites. Worse yet they come into our lives to teach us patience. But everyone brings us some lesson. Take that belief and put it on the next time you face someone that you can't tolerate.

Every event is a blessing. It is just so difficult to see the gift when the wrapping paper is still on. I once was asked by a minister to speak with a lady whose son was an alcoholic. After I said my little piece the minister prayed that God would take control of her son's life. He was asking her to let go and let God. After they spoke awhile about her fear of letting go of the control over the events of her son's life the minister said, "If your son gets drunk and gets a DWI or into an automobile accident we will count that as a blessing too. Right?"

She had to be willing to let any event that precipitated his recovery be a blessing in disguise.

Our blessings are often disguised as events that seem to be tragic. How often I have marveled at a minor illness that has precipitated the discovery of cancer so early that the person survived.

Every heartache is a healing. It was Henry Ward Beecher who said, "God appoints our graces to be nurses to other men's weaknesses."

Sometimes it takes years to see how perfect the unavoidable "tragic event" was. My good friend David Toma told me that the death of his son, and his own struggle with addiction, were wonderful blessings in his life. He will never get over the tragic loss of his son, David Jr. But his death was the single most important event that put him on the road to helping millions of young lives around the world.

Toma still grieves that fateful day. It wasn't until years later that he could see it as preparation for him to be able to help others.

His tragedy was a healing for thousands of teenagers. More often, though, it is a healing for oneself.

Every loss is a hidden gain. We grieve our losses bitterly. I know I have. Yet when we become peaceful rather than get intolerant, we intuitively know that nothing is lost without some gain. It takes a door closing and some frustration to cause you to look for a new one. The gain is there somewhere. You must, however, be willing to look for it. All too often the tendency is to move from intolerance to victimization when confronted by a loss.

Patience is the only virtue you will ever need. I read in a discourse by Sathya Sai Baba that patience is the only virtue you will ever need. That irritated me at first. I was interested in transformation and was reading about spiritual enlightenment. I was not at all interested in learning about patience. It is true, though, that patience is the key. When I came to grips with this idea I wanted to be profoundly patient, immediately. Certainly if you are going to practice releasing the character flaw of intolerance, all you really need is patience. It will give you the wherewithal to see every loss as a hidden gain, every heartache as a healing, and every event as a blessing. Patience will allow you the time to change how you view things. It will help you to judge things not by appearances but on the more profound truths that are attached to them. By that I mean patience will give you the opportunity to see your own stuff and how it contaminates your view of the world. The truth is often a lot simpler than our fantasies of reality. People are usually good intentioned about what they do and why they do things. When you have been wounded deeply enough it takes a long time to learn that there are people you can trust. Be patient to discover trust.

Life is marvelous! Become like little children. Really the most basic differences between adults and children is the capacity to marvel and the capacity to trust. I am a die-hard marveller. I don't even know if that is a word, but I marvel at anything. I look at every human being as totally unique, special, a triumph of God's great imagination. I love to visit foreign lands, eat strange foods, try to speak new languages, because everything is marvelous. I used to marvel at the diseases I saw in medical school. I marvel at character flaws and all they reveal.

Release Is Marvelous

The release of a character flaw really is a marvel to behold. Sometimes when a patient releases one suddenly there is a gush of tears and laughter. More often the release is done lightly. You "let go lightly and hold on tightly" to the virtues you need to replace the character flaw.

I suggest that you practice:

- Tolerance
- Patience
- Acceptance
- Marveling
- Gratitude

So often we use the term "tolerate" to mean we are intolerant but acting like a good victim. You know what I mean. That is not what I intend with the word "tolerance." It feels different than "intolerance," even though on the surface the behaviors can look the same. You have to be willing to hold good motives, demand honesty, and trust in people to be tolerant.

You need patience. Slowly the flaw will leave. It will come back in moments of weakness, but that is just a part of human nature. Instead of being intolerant, be patient, but set up boundaries that are real and very workable. Give relationships time. The longer you are tolerant the more interesting things you will find out about people. Impatience needs to be corrected with tranquillity. Be patient with yourself too. You didn't develop your flaws overnight. Don't demand that they get removed overnight either. Sometimes that happens, but not often. Correct yourself and deal with the uneasy feelings.

Be disciplined about it. You have to consistently and persistently give yourself acceptance. You have to patiently give it to others too. Acceptance sometimes is not easy. I know. I have had to maintain a nonjudgmental attitude toward some of the most difficult people on the planet. I found it difficult during my forensic rotation in residency when I had to interview murderers. One night in a group at my office a patient admitted to having murdered someone while intoxicated. The patient had no recall. Something inside me cried for the patient and the victim. He had been clean and sober for years but never forgiven himself.

Why should I put up with that other person's stuff, you may ask. I'll give you Benjamin Franklin's response, "He is not well-bred, that cannot bear ill-breeding in others."

Often it is adversity in life that causes us to develop great character. Intolerance is the inability to endure hardship. Develop toughness and seek to discover your own inner resources. Then practice marveling at what you have been endowed with. It's all there. Everything you need to respond to an adversity and come through a better person for it is within you. Practice marveling at the small things in life and you will eventually see that life is a joy to live, not a burden to tolerate.

Marveling allows you to experience gratitude. Your heart knows no virtue that is more humbling and more profound than deep gratitude. All the character flaws are afraid of gratitude. If you have deep character flaws, gratitude is difficult. Yet there is so much that we need to be grateful for in order to be human. It is as difficult to acknowledge gratitude as it is to do a good deed. Learn to feel and express gratitude. Make a list of all that you have to be grateful for, and on the days die-hard intolerance has taken over, stop and read it. Hopefully it will bring you back to your senses.

The Poor Me or Martyr Syndrome

HOW DO YOU KNOW IF YOU HAVE *THE POOR ME OR MARTYR SYNDROME?*

1. Are you involved in one or more abusive relationships?

2. Do you believe that people owe you special treatment because you are a victim?

3. Are you famous for getting others to participate in your misery?

4. Do you believe that outside forces control you?

5. Do you believe that you are better than those who victimize you?

6. Do you believe being a martyr gives you the right to blame people?

7. Do you believe that being a victim puts you in an elite group?

8. Have you returned to situations where you are victimized more than once?

9. Do you like to get people to make up to you after they have harmed you?

10. Do you love to be rescued?

11. Do you love to rescue and then get angry when the other person doesn't appreciate your help?

12. Does staying in abusive situations make you morally superior?

13. Do you constantly talk about your misery?

14. Do you blur your current misery with past trauma?

15. Do you believe that you suffer unnecessarily but no one appreciates you for it?

16. Do you ask for help from qualified experts and then don't follow their advice?

17. Have you been promising yourself that you will get out of the abuse situation sometime soon?

18. When you whine, do you believe you have a right to do it?

19. Do you make amends to others or only focus on what amends they can make to you?

Have you ever wondered what drives some sorry souls back into the same abusive relationship over and over again? Have you ever wondered how some women manage to find the same jerk to date or marry only in a different body? You see victims everywhere. They are not dunces or particularly foolish. Their victimization is evidence that a character flaw is at work. It is sad, even tragic. Character flaws are no respecters of intelligence.

For years I have listened to some of the saddest stories of abuse, from people who find themselves in situations of trauma and pain.

Where others, who lack any real respect for life, use and then cast aside those whom they have hurt. I make absolutely no excuses for the victimizer. I have an especially severe attitude with child abusers, molesters, and rapists. I have to temper my intolerance when confronted by patients who abuse their spouses and have no remorse or guilt.

Those who abuse usually can't learn without severe and abrupt punishment. I am not trying to be harsh and unforgiving about this, simply realistic. You can't communicate with someone who has a severe character flaw by normal means. It is too bad that these abusers have an uncanny ability to find victims—not just anyone to victimize, but unfortunates who suffer from the martyr syndrome.

So let me be up front about it. There are a host of victims out there who have truly suffered. They deserve our compassion and our support. How then do you distinguish between an innocent victim and one who suffers from the martyr syndrome? If you know people who are using their victimization in a way that disrupts relationships and creates chaos, they are flawed. If you see people who are trying to embellish their victimization or set themselves up as victims, then they are flawed. If you know someone whose idea of fun is to have a pity party, you've got the picture.

Maybe you know someone who is miserable and tries to get everyone else to participate in the misery so that he can be the center of attention. Then you know this flaw. If you see the saintly sucker who runs back into the fires of hell to make sure she has been burned enough to warrant your sympathies, then you have met a martyr. This is a person who deliberately plays the role of the sacrificial lamb. Let's take a look at this misery for what it is, a desperate grab for power, control, and sympathy.

Misery Loves Power

Misery doesn't love company but recognition. People who invite misery set themselves up to be sacrificed. Being a martyr is a good thing, right? It got the early Christians into heaven. Today's martyrs suffer needlessly at the hands of the psychopaths that they have decided to rescue. Here is a typical scenario:

Proud Mary, a young nurse, met a police officer whom she claimed had a "slight" hand problem. She came to my office because she wanted to save the relationship. She stared across the desk at me through tearful eyes. The makeup on her face ran. She should have used waterproof mascara. Mary couldn't hide the black eye.

> If misery loves company, misery has company enough.
> —HENRY DAVID THOREAU

She had been immediately infatuated with her cop's gregarious, outgoing personality and his self-assuredness. No one intimidated him. He carried his gun well and she was proud to be his woman.

After a while they fought. She found out that his drinking was a little more of a problem than it first seemed, but not enough to try and get him into a program. She didn't want to hurt his chances for promotion, so she covered for him. Even though his own friends warned her that he was "rough" with everyone, including women, she thought she could fix him. She had the fantasy that in the crucible of her love she could stir his stuff and transform it into virtue. She would be recognized as the woman who finally tamed the wild passions of this man. It turned out her face wasn't as tough as his fists.

Misery doesn't love company but belonging. Judy was a rebel without a home but had a lot of outlandish causes to pursue. She was a victim who was pathologically loyal. She was tough and liked danger, dangerous men, and excitement. After a series of disastrous relationships she finally met the biker of her dreams. When she became pregnant and suddenly wanted to have a home in which to raise the child, her biker "friend" decided to leave. She found out that all his promises of loyalty were really loyalty to his needs. She based her victimization on a need to be part of a group and to show fierce loyalty. Once the baby came she crashed emotionally.

Misery doesn't love company but freedom. Mark was a minister whose wife liked younger men. In fact that is why she married him. He knew he was in trouble from the beginning but refused to leave the relationship. He craved freedom, and yet wanted to be taken care of. He sacrificed himself for a woman who repeatedly humiliated him with her boy toys. She promised to be more discreet and even told him, "This time I'm stopping the insanity. No more. Trust me." He believed her or at least needed to believe her. Mark vowed to show the members of his church that prayer and patience could change anyone. In therapy he admitted that he really didn't want her to change. He loved the idea that he was a martyr at the matrimonial altar. He prided himself on being the perfect victim. It liberated him to admonish all those who didn't suffer as well as he did.

Misery doesn't love company but fun. Andrea confessed to me that she was willing to risk all the problems related to her promiscuity as long as she could still have fun. She didn't see herself as a victim of sexual abuse or as a survivor of rape. The memories had been repressed. Her acting out, though, had been a direct result of the damage done by an evil uncle. Now she just wanted to have fun, even if she had to make herself everybody's sexual target.

Misery loves a pity party. Misery loves company as long as the company is going to take care of the needs of the victim. Without the proper recognition a lot of sufferers of the victim syndrome would quit and go find something better to do. They usually don't because the rewards are too high.

Misery loves to see you suffer. I can't finish this section without commenting on the movie *Misery*. If you haven't seen it, go watch it after reading this chapter. Kathy Bates will give you great insight into the most important need of the victim. That need is to victimize other people. She has to make other people suffer, to create misery, because she sees herself as a victim.

This character flaw creates a noble martyr who decides it's her duty to deliver the wrath of God.

In the Company of Martyrs

What are the true benefits to being a martyr? It really is quite simple. You are sanctified. When people's sick beliefs support playing the role of sacrificial lamb they believe that they have become a saint. The early Christian martyrs are the classic example of this. They were filled with joy and power. Because they suffered and died for Christ and His church, they were canonized. Now take that same principle and bring it to the twentieth century, take away the joy, the spirituality, add a large dose of ego, and you have the martyr syndrome. You have people who maintain the illusion that saying "poor me" brings dignity and respect.

Their beliefs are similar except the early Christians elevated themselves to the role of Christ. If you peel off the layers of belief that cover the poor-me types' true intentions you will eventually get to anger. It is as intense as raging indignation, but used differently. They hope to make their partner look bad or feel guilty. They see their suffering as proof that they are good. It is just a character flaw, however, contaminating a person's life, using misery to hang on to self-esteem. Sacrificial lambs use the character flaw to take power and control others.

Their hidden agenda is "I'll make you feel so bad! You'll be sorry you ever victimized me!"

Strolling Down the Street of Sorrows

If the martyrs in your life had started out as mean and nasty individuals it would be easy to point out their crazy behavior. They don't, however, and that makes it so much harder to be objective about them. We have a human need to show compassion for the victimized and the abused. Pointing out their "stuff" should always be done as gently as possible so that they can make some corrections. It should never be done with the attitude of criticism or rejection. Sacrificial lambs have already sacrificed enough. They don't need further abuse from us, but they do need to have their patterns of abuse interrupted whenever we see them.

Everyone who uses this character flaw has actually been victimized in the past. Usually it was real trauma. Whether it was real or only a false recall syndrome doesn't make too much of a difference in how you treat the present situation. The past episodes of abuse, real or not, are used to abuse people in the present. If the victim is creating chaos rather than healing old wounds, then the character flaw is operating.

Keeping Balance by Suffering

Johnny Skateboard was a young loner who had been beaten by his father repeatedly as a child. He lived with his mom and sisters. Usually he hung out and used his skateboard as an escape. His father was a trucker who was frequently away. Johnny always made sure he was home when his father came back. He would immediately take the brunt of his father's wrath.

In therapy Johnny recalled seeing his mother abused by his drunken father. She had been beaten and raped while little Johnny tried to keep the other children hidden in the bedroom. He admitted that he thought he could keep his father from beating his mother if he bore the brunt of the violence.

Johnny really believed that he could keep a balance in the family by suffering. It all blew up when he refused to set himself up anymore. Chaos erupted, but it signified a new equilibrium based on healing.

St. Mama My Hero!

Children want to grow up to be just like their parents. When one of your parents was a victim and the other a practitioner of raging indignation you have a problem. Emotional chains are set up. These are not chains that hold you down but chains that link feelings. The son or daughter of an abusive parent will start to link kindness to accepting abuse. There will be a chaining together of passivity with nobility. All sorts of crazy emotional baggage will be created. Often the adult who becomes a victim was the witness of abuse and not the physical recipient of it. But the links to the chain were set in place. When an abusive situation occurs the chains of emotional chaos are ready to hold the abused in the role of victim.

What makes this so difficult for some to accept is that the victim may not need to play victim because of the situation but simply because the chain of emotions is running automatically.

Mike, a sensitive young man, came in for counseling because he was having fantasies of beating his wife. He had never hit a woman before and thought he was going crazy. After a few sessions it became apparent that his wife, who had been badly traumatized as a child, was angry with him. She was trying to get him to hurt her. She went into counseling too, and a tragedy was avoided.

The Core of the Matter

Mike's wife, whose mother had been abused, was angry. It is often the core emotion but can't be acted upon. Saints don't get angry. Martyrs suffer in silence. Sacrificial lambs don't want to look at their core issues and beliefs. They see themselves as onions. You peel an onion and cry. There is nothing in the center. It is never their fault. With true victims, I'll buy that. With this character flaw they are more like artichokes. Peel it down layer by layer, and just before you get to the tender heart of the matter, there is a very delicate area covered with thorns.

It's not easy to get to a victim's heart. All such individuals' patterns are learned defenses. They don't want to give them up. What happens, though, when you get to their core is that you discover the martyr's operating rules.

Martyr's Rules!

If you could control the feelings of everyone else in your world, would it be worth it? Probably not, but don't tell the martyrs, they might get angry. Actually they already are angry, but now they might show it. Then you might not feel sorry for them and like them so much. Here are the rules. See how many you believe too.

- Outside forces control me
- I am special
- I am better than the victimizer
- I belong to an elite group
- I should get to control the amends
- It's not my fault—now I can blame
- Now I have the right to be angry. I am livid

Outside forces control me. This is a fundamental belief carried by victims of this character flaw—the outside world is in control of their life. Often it is difficult to distinguish between a true victim and one who has the victim syndrome. The difference is so subtle that it has to be closely dissected. At the same time you must cut away the beliefs that damage the character and cause further victimization.

This is not as simple as it sounds. Sometimes bad things happen to good people. Often I've had to consult with cancer victims who were depressed and angry about their disease. It is one thing to help a person grieve the loss of his or her life and to make peace with himself or herself. It is a lot more difficult to make a person who has suffered abuse and perpetuated it through crazy relationships look at his or her anger.

This was true of a young lady with lymphoma who was going to die. She had been depressed for quite some time. Her oncologist wanted me to see her because she was crying whenever he visited her. She had been a victim of violent crime and had developed a stress disorder. Later when the cancer took over, her symptoms returned. It seemed like a pretty straightforward case until the social worker informed me that she was married to an abusive husband. The patient had stayed in the relationship for years, angry with her husband. Now she was furious that she had never separated. He was going to "inherit the children."

I am special! We all have that belief from time to time. When you are special, simply because you were created by God, then you are okay. When one of the things that makes you feel special is to be abused or punished, then the character flaw has you. Every now and then you hear stories of people who bought crazy things from scam artists. You hear the same words from them. "I was promised something so unbelievably wonderful that I should have known it wasn't true." Scam artists know how to pick people who are willing victims or simply gullible.

These swindlers prey upon the innocent, using one of the rules that motivates these sacrificial lambs—specialness. They look for people who believe that they are special and offer them a deal. It works this way. First you get something so good that it is almost like stealing. It's something for nothing. Then it turns out that the scam artist has stolen from you. You were robbed because you were special. Now you can play the victim and be special.

I am better than the victimizer. Usually this uniqueness is related to proving that you are better than others and deserve respect and veneration from the rest of us. It is about being a martyr, therefore by your great suffering and sacrifice you have gained a place of honor.

I respect people who make great sacrifice, especially those who don't complain about it. They just try to make the world a better place. What most of us can't tolerate is someone who wants to whine and wallow in self-pity in order to make others feel bad. You know the type: every time you speak with them they are telling you how they have been mistreated. They are saints compared to the sinners who abuse them.

> **I think the most uncomfortable thing about martyrs is that they look down on people who aren't.**
> **—SAMUEL N. BEHRMAN**

Martyrs' self-pity is a kind of eulogy to their suffering. They make sure that they are recognized for the great torment that they have suffered. I wish I could tell the story of one of these patients. I can't. I've seen so many that they've all started sounding the same. "I came, I suffered, and I stayed." These martyrs suffer from a severe superiority complex that depends upon their being unjustly punished to feel righteous. It's such a difficult way to live.

I belong to an elite group. You have heard it before. "The group I belong to is special. We are the not so silent sufferers of the world, looking for other members. Rather than change ourselves we will stay in our situations and perpetuate our suffering. That is, as long as you continue to consider us special and as long as we get some control out of the deal." Okay, maybe they are not that up front about it.

An elderly Italian lady was referred to my office by her internist. She had been in a relationship with a tyrant. He was an old Italian man who modeled his husband role after *Il Duce,* Mussolini. Her husband was proud of the authority he wielded. The children confirmed the situation to me. Her husband was probably incapable of changing, especially since he was addicted to being right. My belief is you can't push a rope, so I didn't try couples therapy with them.

It was actually very simple for me to help this woman. I knew her priest and had him support me in getting her to view her special status as based on her relationship with God and not with her husband. She had to stop seeing herself as part of a group of women who throughout the ages bore the brunt of men's mean character. The priest did something unusual. He explained to her that it was a sin for her to play victim to her husband if God didn't want her to. What a crisis that precipitated! The children confirmed my suspicions. The husband was more willing to change than she was.

You see, she also was obeying the next rule. **I get to control the amends**. Victims get to say how much you need to do in order to make it up to them. When you have harmed a martyr, you go to purgatory and sit out an elaborate punishment. It is designed to empower the victimized and control the victimizer. It is not really about forgiveness and amends, even though on the surface that is what it is supposed to be about. It is about making someone else suffer like you have. Remember the woman who stayed in her marriage to punish her husband. "You will suffer like I do, and I will determine when it is enough."

It is very difficult to make up to someone when you have harmed them. It is even harder when the person you are asking forgiveness from plans to rub your nose in it. You have to control your guilt and resentment at the same time. The martyr controls how much guilt you feel, or at least hopes to. Sacrificial lambs go to slaughter blaming others for their being stuck in a situation that they could have ended.

> Had we not faults of our own, we should take less pleasure in complaining of others.
> —FRANÇOIS DE SALIGNAC DE LA MOTHE FÉNELON

"It's not my fault!—now I can blame." Chronic victims may not say that they want to blame others, but they do all the time. It is one of the most consistent rewards of being a victim. The victimized get to point the finger. Naturally I don't intend to minimize responsibility for the person who is participating in this insanity, but I also don't excuse people who put themselves in harm's way just so they can point the finger at someone else.

When people use the fact that they have been victimized so that they can enjoy assigning blame, then they are merry martyrs. The merriment is just an illusion. They whine and blame and try to get others to suffer. It may not be physical punishment, but it is emotional battery. Underneath it all is the core, anger.

Now they have the right to be angry. Finally the passive victim, the suffering martyr, has reached the goal. **He or she has the right to be angry and is livid**. Every true saint seeks peace, but this "mad" martyr is looking for an opportunity to use raging indignation and not get caught. The melancholy martyr is looking to feel angry and abused, yet still be exalted in the eyes of others.

Real saints pray for forgiveness. This type of chronic victim secretly seeks vengeance. Be careful with them, because they will extract their pound of flesh for your ounce of abuse.

The Martyr on Main Street

Douglas, a former owner of a trucking firm, came to see me about his heroin addiction. He was seriously ill and required a detoxification. While working with him in group he told us a remarkable story. He claimed he was the victim of psychological abuse from the DEA. Apparently they had started surveillance of his trucking operation because of his drug use. Someone had tipped them off that he was dealing. Since Doug wasn't dealing, he felt he was being persecuted by them. He believed that they were interfering in his ability to manage his trucking company. He became indignant and confronted their surveillance team. He got into a fight and was arrested. He was a victim, right?

The idea of people thinking they are victims has spread like cancer through our society. Our criminal justice system has turned prisoners' rights into an opportunity for criminals to play martyr. It is pervasive. In Doug's case, his therapy group wouldn't put up with his rationalizing. They kept pointing out how he was victimizing himself with the drugs, society with his tax evasion, and the group with that lamebrained story. It is quite obvious to people from outside our culture that we take better care of the criminals than we do of their victims, by allowing the criminal to play victim.

We Love to Rescue a Victim

Martyrs know that we love "the rescue." It is exciting and has many rewards. Being rescued proves you are better than the victimizer. Being a rescuer puts you into a special group of saviors. That makes you as close to being a saint as you will ever come. The recognition is fantastic, and sometimes it starts out as fun.

Rescuing victims isn't as much fun as it is cracked up to be. True victims are a blessing to help, but the martyr will torture you and abuse you, since you are the only one available. Most of the victimized don't travel a pretty path. It is littered with broken relationships, physical trauma, emotional abuse, and economic problems. They walk their path trying to fill some deep need. Worst of all, most of it could have been avoided with a little common sense and a desire not to participate in insane behavior.

One of the most difficult things for a therapist to do is to be patient while trying to help a martyr give up being victimized. I have had counselors come to me furious with their clients' behavior. Just when they thought there had been some change, the pattern would reccur. The counselor would then feel used and abused.

Women fall into the abused category more frequently than men. Children are more likely to be victimized than adults. But the character flaw shows up in both men and women. Rescuers tend to use the flaw more often than abusers, but everybody has the capacity to use it.

O Those Marriages from Hell!

I said in a previous chapter that victims often attach themselves to the raging indignant. That, without a doubt, is a marriage made in hell. When the character flaw is pointed out to someone who has been repeatedly abused, the common response is to go back to the abuser, confront him, and get abused again. Counselors often jump through hoops to help women get to a battered shelter. If you have been abused and are now out of the relationship, do some volunteer work at a shelter.

Frequently when the rescue mechanism was in place the victim would opt to stay in the abusive relationship. The needs are so great that they have to return. There can be layers of old issues that are locked together. The further victimization "feels" like it is breathing life into a hopeless situation. Sometimes the character flaw is the true cause of death. It was Oscar Wilde who said, "A thing is not necessarily true because a man dies for it." A relationship that a woman dies for is not love but living hell. If you are in an abusive relationship get help, and do it quickly.

More often the abuse is less severe. It is emotional battery tolerated to fulfill frustrated desires. One of my patients, Dee, stayed married to keep her little idyllic family together. She couldn't stand her husband, yet in her first few sessions she defended his abuse and intolerance as staunchly as you would defend high character. Dee's husband reminded her of her father. The demeaning intolerance and the resentment felt normal. She stayed until it escalated to physical abuse.

For many of my patients the confrontation over staying in a tortured relationship has great religious significance for them. Dee was a Roman Catholic who suddenly realized what her priest meant when he kept telling her that she should consider the possibility of an annulment. The old priest told her, "Marriages aren't made in hell. This can't be a marriage if the two of you weren't spiritually united."

It is easy to spot the marriages that are real. The couple will engage in a real effort to release their character flaws. Each welcomes and celebrates the change in his or her partner. They also don't consider divorce a first option. Personal transformation is the option. Victims and their victimizers have a "scrap" button. When things go wrong, as they often do, they suddenly abandon the relationship. It is all or none.

Sometimes the martyr develops a real sickness, like depression or Posttraumatic Stress Disorder (PTSD). It is hard to get a spouse to understand that the martyr is really sick, not crying wolf. Spouses are sometimes so used to hearing "poor me" from the martyr that they assume it's all part of the chronic pattern.

Wendy came to my office after a car accident. "I was in a collision and I am acting crazy," she said to me. At first I thought she was referring to neurological damage of some sort. "I have anxiety attacks and feel like I am being picked on by everyone."

She was a survivor of incest and had experienced many episodes of abuse in her first marriage. She had been happily married for a number of years after working on her issues. The accident triggered classic symptoms of PTSD, which didn't respond well to treatment. Her need to play victim to her present husband also kicked in. She was distressed at finding herself disrupting the relationship even when nothing was going on between them.

> **If you suffer, thank God! It is a sure sign that you are alive.**
> **—ELBERT HUBBARD**

During the course of her therapy she had to deal with the episodes of abuse at the hands of her first husband all over again. She also had to resolve her suppressed grief over an abortion she had when she was younger.

Wendy hadn't simply fallen back into the pattern of martyr but had responded to the new trauma too. Her problem was that the old patterns took over quickly and brought her right back to "those old feelings." Wendy was a "punisher." She tried hard to make other people feel guilty when she believed she had been "wronged."

Misery Is Optional

Suffering is not something that you can easily avoid. Life is tough. Bad things will happen even to the nicest people. Suffering is not optional, but misery is. This is an important point to remember when working on releasing the martyr complex. You don't necessarily need to be miserable when you are suffering. I know that sounds a bit extreme, but think about how many times you have watched someone go through something unavoidable and not complain. Contrast that with the martyr who is looking for sympathy, self-pity, or to extract a victim's revenge.

I remember a young lady who came to my office one day to discuss her feelings of rage toward her ex-boyfriend. She described a classic rage-aholic who was addicted to being right. He pursued her at work, where a number of the other men offered to have him meet with an accident. He felt powerless in the breakup of their relationship and she felt powerless in confronting him.

Sometimes it is difficult to understand how sick these people are, based on secondhand information, but the character she was describing seemed terribly abusive. He later attacked her in her parents' house in front of the children. Often the victimized will hook up with men who disregard orders of protection. They are sociopaths who couldn't care less about law and order. As part of a strategy to empower her, my patient decided to take lessons in self-defense and to carry pepper spray as a deterrent.

She finally came to realize that the misery was optional. She understood that a lot of really wonderful people experience traumas and suffer, but the misery wasn't necessary. She worked hard at her self-defense, and as did many of my battered patients she became very adept at using her spray.

He was sorry the next time he tried to attack her. She wasn't lucky, she was prepared.

How to Peel the Layers

Peeling the layers of protection from one's ego can sometimes be hazardous. As you may have already surmised, these sacrificial lambs frequently find themselves in situations that are more than abusive. They are actually dangerous. Change has to be undertaken at a pace that ensures safety. Contacts with shelters or social services must be readily available.

More often than not, though, the martyr is not so much in physical as in emotional danger. The goal of the martyr is to try and salvage self-esteem by demonstrating that she or he has a right to say poor me. The abuse is set up to prove self-worth or to take care of some deep need. This was true of a woman in a codependency group who claimed that she had been used by a married man. The group had listened to this single woman's stories of dating men who were safe because they were married. She picked men who couldn't or wouldn't commit to a serious relationship. Then she set it up to get dumped so that she could whine about it. It took a long time for her to face her own fear of commitment. It was a layer that was hard to remove. Without facing that fear, the victimization would have continued.

When you have a friend who plays victim, be careful. Tread lightly. Often there is so much pain associated with victimization that it is difficult to touch on. You have to be cautious. Patterns are best broken with support, not just insight.

Separate Out the Issues from Reality

It is difficult to hear what the issues are with a victim. The next time a martyr starts to explain why he or she is so miserable listen for which issues relate to the present situation. Then see what is related to the past. It will fascinate you because often they blur. The past and the present are all one. Watch the flow of emotion. Events will seem cyclical and not linear. What happened last month and today are blended.

The issues for a victim are those old beliefs that "I suffer unnecessarily. I must be better than others. No one suffers quite like I do." Then notice the link to the past episodes of trauma. "I have always suffered. Have pity on me in my misery." You may not be able to do much with the issues, but you can focus on the present reality.

Should you pity the martyr? That may be the entire goal of the victim syndrome. All the person may be trying to do is to find out if anyone still cares for them. Pity is not necessarily caring. Often it is a way of jumping into other's character flaws with them. It is better to change one belief than it is to spend time with pity.

Is the Suffering Necessary?

Ask people if their suffering is necessary. If they say yes, then ask what is the lesson it will teach them. If they say that they don't know ask them to think about it for a while. Some will say no. Ask them why they are continuing. If they are really learning something, then all is not lost, and they can give up being miserable. If they are not learning anything, then why are they staying in the situation? Their answer is always that it is out of their control.

PUT YOUR PATTERNS ON PAUSE!

- Safety first

- Control what you can

- Stop complaining

- Look for meaning

- Stay focused on the present

- Make amends
- Empower yourself
- Practice forgiveness
- Give service

Safety first. Since martyrs will put themselves in harm's way and often not have the support to get out, focus on safety first. As a resident I met the first of my battered patients. She couldn't leave her home because she couldn't figure out where to go. Then, I thought it was unusual. Now I know better. If safety is an issue, do something immediately.

Control what you can. If you are inviting victimization upon yourself, then make the changes that will stop it. Do it immediately. Remind yourself that the misery is optional. Most of what victims waste their time on is out of their control. There can never be any peace trying to gain control of something that you can't master. It isn't like learning a talent, where even a little accomplishment is better than nothing. What the martyr is doing is more like trying to control the weather. If you don't like the climate where you are, stop complaining and move. You can control where you are. You can't change others. You may demand that others change, but you can't force them. You can make others suffer the consequences of their behavior, but you can't control the behavior. Sometimes you can't even control the consequences, just your response. So focus on what you can control.

Stop complaining. This is the hardest part of the cure. So often victims stay victimized so that they have the right to complain. Give it up. Stop complaining for the next twenty-four hours. Do it one day at a time and see what happens. Your friends won't recognize your voice when you take the whine out of it.

Look for meaning. It is related to beliefs about yourself that you picked up as an abused child, or from witnessing the abuse of others.

Whatever the meaning of the abuse for you, work on learning from it and moving on. Most of the time you will find that the real meaning is that you have to grow up and let go of the crazy beliefs others gave you. Victims seem to run in families, just as abuse does. If you have a family belief about the meaning of life that says you deserve to be miserable, give it up. Sometimes it is very difficult to grow up and adopt your own beliefs.

Stay focused on the present. If you find yourself slipping into the whining, complaining misery that accompanies this flaw, stop and pull yourself into the present. Chances are that you are slipping into the past and into the future. You are trying to feel good about both. It is okay to suffer and learn. It is okay to pass through difficulties and grow, but you can't go lump your past misery and future fears on a bad situation and gain any insight on it.

Ask yourself if you really need to be considered a saint right now. Do you want people to feel sorry for you and acknowledge your suffering or do you want to do something about it?

Remind yourself that the world praises dead saints and persecutes the living. Do you absolutely need that right now? If you do, okay, but if you don't, look for what you need now.

A Simple Cure!

Actually there is a lot that you can do to change your life if you suffer with this character flaw. First, recognize that your life is exactly where it needs to be because this is the reality that is facing you. Practice honesty and acceptance of the situation and get ready to move on. You will start to move on if and when you become accountable for your part in the victimization.

I can remember a patient screaming in outrage at me. "I have no part in it, Doc. It is all his fault. That miserable, uncompassionate . . ." The rest was a little too abusive to report here. She was incensed that I could even insinuate that she was responsible for the situation she was in.

"Maybe you could start by admitting that you should not be in another relationship for a while," I said after she settled down. "I don't condone his actions, but you don't control him. Maybe you could stop meeting guys at bars."

Accountability rather than rights, again. Personal accountability is fundamental to releasing flaws. The second part to changing this pattern is to make amends.

Mend Your Character Flaw with Amends

Remember that victims seek to control amends, not make them. Before you get turned off to the idea, hear me out on this peculiar thought. For me, making amends is taking the virtue you lacked and practicing it in the relationship that was damaged.

For instance, a victim of abuse is often dishonest and stays in relationships that are horrible. She will lie to herself and pretend that it is okay. The first amends she needs to make are to herself. She does that when she is honest about the relationship. If it stinks, admit it.

A chronic whiner may be looking for sympathy so that she can be the center of attention. The amends she needs to bring to her friends are peacefulness. Pay more attention to others.

Another martyr might be trying to keep her husband pitying her so that she will be sainted, viewed as better than others. She needs to look for the good qualities of others and point them out. She needs to take the focus off herself.

By constantly seeking to make amends for our behavior we dis-empower the character flaw and empower our character.

Groups Are Great

Victims usually need to work in group therapy and attend support groups. We survive together and help one another transform in group. Groups are great for calling us on our "stuff." We should form groups only to empower the individual, not to control the outside. Often the opposite happens. People in groups try to control those who have damaged us and force them to be punished. I have no problem with the punishment, but it is not a cure for you, just the natural consequence of fulfilling your duty to society. If you want to change, then the group should be about your response, not the fate of others.

Forgiveness Will Unlock Your Power

So much of your power is tied up in being a victim. Unleashing that power requires forgiving the aggressor and moving on. Forgiveness does not mean letting a person go without being accountable. It means letting go of the belief that the other person has ultimate control. I have seen so many innocent victims of accidents move on once they have forgiven the person who hurt them. Often it was a parent or sibling driving the car. The forgiveness was the key to getting one's life back. More often than not the angry victim is furious at himself or herself for allowing the victimization. Admitting that doesn't forgive the perpetrator but releases you from the self-hatred that will keep you a prisoner forever unless you deal with it.

Sometimes people get away with evil.

Accept it. On the superficial level it seems that sometimes people get away with it. Sometimes there is nothing you can do about it. When you can't do anything about it, learn and move on. It will seem less significant to you in the years to come if you let go now.

The Magic of Service

The final stage of release from this flaw is to get involved in selfless service. That is service to others with absolutely no focus on any gain, recognition, or reward for you. This is the complete opposite of the flaw. It is a state of mind that brings the opposite feeling too.

When you are involved in total loving service you will experience joy, peace, and fulfillment. Sometimes it will feel even better than that. And things don't have to be going well for you to experience it.

Let me explain how I came to this conclusion. I have had the good fortune to know half a dozen missionaries who have worked in India, Africa, and Mexico. They all were amazing in their ability to tolerate great hardship. Each of them would eventually have to take a break from what they were doing when they would start to burn out. They could tell they needed rest and relaxation when they started feeling victimized by their circumstances. It was always the same pattern. The selfless individuals felt wonderful, fully alive, giving to people who had no way to repay them. The circumstances were horrible, yet the experience was extremely rewarding. It made no difference how bad things were. They were fulfilled.

Service works the opposite of victimization. You go from thinking about your rights and how you were wronged to seeing how much you can truly help others. Service allows people to change from a victim to an empowered servant of humanity.

If you decide that you are ready to let go of this character flaw and get involved in service you will need a good dose of humility. Only the humble serve. When service is done out of vanity all you have really done is gone from victim to grandiosity. When victims let go of whining so that they can be considered heroes, they are letting their self-regard run riot over everyone else. That's another flaw and the stuff of the next chapter.

Self-regard Run Riot

HOW DO YOU KNOW IF YOU HAVE *SELF-REGARD RUN RIOT?*

1. Are you one of the chosen few who should have more say in how the world is run?

2. Do you justify selfish behavior with the rationalization that you are taking care of yourself?

3. Do you constantly focus on your own needs because it is a sign of moral superiority?

4. Are you greedy or jealous or do you put down others who have more than you?

5. Do you wear unique-ers, i.e., do you think you are totally unique?

6. Do you believe that everyone should or better yet would like you?

7. Are you so self-absorbed that you think self-regard is self-esteem?

8. Do you spend a lot time before a mirror and is that where you have your most intense conversations?

9. Do you like to tell people how good you are at something rather than show them?

10. Do you embellish the truth so that you seem more interesting?

11. After you abuse or walk over someone do you explain how it was good for them?

12. Do you believe that being selfish is normal for an adult?

13. Are your emotions more important than others'?

14. When people ask how you are, do you give them a really long answer and think it's interesting?

15. Do you feel you need and have a right to have an affair?

16. Do you feel you are underappreciated?

17. Do your ends justify your means?

18. Do you always have the best of intentions even when you do things that are wrong?

19. Do you feel that you have the right to cheat or cut corners?

I was in a shuttle van going to a gala affair during the Christmas season many years ago. We were all dressed up in formal wear, looking very pretty. I was doing my normal self-aggrandizing rap about what a cool guy I was. Back then I still thought M. D. after my name was Latin for *Maximus Deus*, or Maximum Deity. This woman in the back of the van listened to me for a while and then couldn't tolerate my braggadocio style any longer. She said, "There is not enough room in this van for you and your ego, mister." That's how I met my wife, Barbara.

I have this secret belief that marriage was instituted by God as a divine tool to reduce the size of the egos of the two partners. But that's another story.

Self-regard run riot, or IR^3 (I are cubed) is one of those natural phenomena that manage to grow without any help from anyone. I call it IR^3 because the people who have this character flaw start most of their sentences with the I are's. They desperately want you to see what and who they are. "I" is their favorite word. Sometimes it shows its face as grandiosity, other times as false humility. Both ways you know the person is trying to impress you. It amounts to pride, false pride to be more exact. False pride is using pride or selfishness to maintain a character flaw.

You're So Vain I'll Bet You Think This Book Is About You!

Of course it is about you. It is about me and you and everyone who walks the face of the earth. It's just that some of us have more intense character flaws than others. There are some people who are so selfish that the church father Tertullian had them in mind when he said, "He who lives only to benefit himself confers on the world a benefit when he dies." You know the type. They are so self-absorbed that they think the world rotates around them and not the sun. This character flaw, or IR^3, is not the same as narcissistic personality, though it is fundamental to that personality. It is not limited to it. Selfishness is part of a basic survival mechanism. We all develop little egos that are responsible for helping us integrate into society. Our egos help us function as separate entities and survive in a complex, interdependent world.

Self-regard run riot is an exaggeration of the basic tendency to explore and find yourself unique, special. It becomes a character flaw when we use self-regard as a justification for being arrogant, selfish, and self-centered. IR^3 is a character flaw that serves as a common pathway for the other flaws. Selfish people are willing to be dishonest if it serves their purpose. Selfishness will enhance addicted to being right. Selfish people are more likely to feel victimized. When you selfishly use behaviors or have thoughts that perpetuate your flaws, you have self-regard running riot in your life. As blatant selfishness, or masked as false humility, this character flaw keeps feeding the others.

Wearing My Unique-ers

We had a pet expression in my office; "He's wearing his unique-ers." It referred to anyone who felt he or she was so special, such a big deal, so cool, wonderful, fabulous . . . Should I go on or do you know the type? Their egos are so puffed up that they bump into everyone when they walk into a room. Or it doesn't fit into the van!

These people like to enter grand hallways, big ballrooms, and expansive foyers because it gives them enough room for their swollen heads. I loved this type in therapy. Their egos were like large balloons. They deflated so easily. Not that deflating egos was my job. Expanding self was. Egos deflate by themselves. Character and virtue expands self. An ego puffs up until it bursts or someone with this character flaw comes around and sticks a pin in it.

This flaw doesn't just present itself as grandiose self-regard. Sometimes it expresses itself as envy or jealousy, wishing that they were better than you. Sometimes the IR[3] looks like arrogance, that they are better than you, and sometimes it's just being overly self-absorbed. You've seen this type—the sun rises and falls only on them.

The Many Faces of Greed

Low self-esteem creates a feeling of lack. One of the ways to compensate for low self-worth is to brag about yourself or try to accumulate stuff. That is to develop false pride and become greedy.

Greed is not just related to money but to other things that cater to the senses. Lust is one of those things. So are thoughtlessness, envy, and arrogance.

Once you recognize that false pride and greed operate through this flaw you will see its many faces. Do you know others who are compulsive overeaters? Often it is shame, guilt, and a number of other flaws that drive these persons. Chances are, though, that you will find a good dose of self-regard run riot driving them to be dishonest about their eating habits. What about lazy people who think everybody else owes them? We all know at least a couple of them. More often, though, we associate greed with the Scrooge McDuck character and Ebeneezer Scrooge from Dickens's *Christmas Carol*.

Character Weeds

In the garden of human character there are many weeds. Self-absorption is the most common. You see, just like garden weeds, these emotional weeds need absolutely no nurturing to grow. Flawed character, however, nurtures self-regard as though it were a very valuable crop. It develops its "gifts" or special abilities at an early age and then works on them throughout life. Unless this aggrandized ego meets with some adversity to temper its growth, it will progress to smugness, cockiness, and eventually to narcissistic conceit. It speaks in glowing terms about itself. Yet it is basically dishonest and lies without knowing it is doing so.

> The man who lives by himself and for himself is likely to be corrupted by the company he keeps.
> —CHARLES H. PARKHURST

These character weeds are everywhere. They feed on negative attitudes and evil thoughts, especially about other people. That may seem strange, since their hyperbole is often so upbeat and positive.

Showmanship and Show-offs

When Muhammad Ali would say, "I am the greatest," we all knew he could back it up with his fists. He was the greatest of his time. He was the greatest showman to hit boxing in years. He revitalized a dying sport. Showmanship is essential in entertainment. That's not the character flaw in action, it is a mature actor pretending to have the flaw in order to provide entertainment.

Living a Lie

Often people want to be considered cool, interesting, and unique. That leads to embellishing the truth and living a lie.

Most of us know people who can't back up half of what they talk about. They are all talk and no performance. They are suffering from inadequacy but think they have to compensate for it with pomposity. These are the haughty self-promoters who want to be worshiped by others. They often have little groups of "fans" who follow them around. When they do reach success they develop large fan clubs and nurture a dependence on their hype. The goal of all their self-promotion is to feed their own ego. It is not to help others improve.

But, you may say, "Isn't selfishness a normal part of life? Isn't it natural?"

Yes, in fact it is for little children. You may have noticed, however, that one of the very first things we teach little children is to share. When do we start? Probably with toddlers, but we get serious about it at three and a half to four years old. That's the same age when their little egos are starting to develop. After four years old we demand that kids cooperate and work together. So if you are older than four and still believe you have a right to be totally selfish and self-centered, I have some advice. Grow up!

Stunted Spiritual Growth

This bizarre fascination with one's own self is an epidemic in our society. We have a cultlike focus on personality, celebrity, and fame. People crave to be in the limelight. As a society we ask, "Are you taking care of yourself? That's what is ultimately important." Yet most other cultures know that you have to be able to take care of others as a measure of your maturity. Our magazines are no longer *Look, Life*, and *National Geographic*. They are *People* and *Self*. This narrowing of our focus reflects stunted spiritual growth. Stunted spiritual growth is deeper and more serious than stunted emotional growth. Your soul is fundamentally more important than your emotions. So if you were reading this book hoping only to deal with some emotional needs, I've got news for you. If you want a transformation in character you have to have spiritual growth.

The term "spiritual growth" means different things for different people. One day a man came into my office concerned that he was losing his mind. He'd had an experience of oneness with God that was so profound it left his ego reeling for weeks. He had merged into God and had a profound mystical experience. In order for him to see it as a spiritual experience and not psychosis he had to read the biographies of Christian mystics. For him spiritual growth was far different than the notion of a young man coming to grips with the character flaw of dishonesty.

Spiritual growth for another may involve understanding the great sacrifice of self that it takes to be a loving mother. For someone else it may mean relearning the religion of one's childhood but with the mature view of an adult. Whatever it is for you, most spiritual growth starts with a dose of truth interfering with a grandiose ego. Rest assured that deflating an overblown ego will create spiritual growth. It is a great place to start.

FEELINGS ASSOCIATED WITH STUNTED SPIRITS

- They feel that their needs aren't being met adequately
- The feel that they need more aggrandizement
- They feel that they suffer from their inadequacy
- They feel that their needs are more important than everyone else's
- They feel that they need to have an affair
- They feel that they need to cheat
- They feel that they are not appreciated
- They feel that they have more of a destiny than others
- They feel that their ends justify their means

I could go on, but you get the point. These individuals have failed to make the normal switch from selfishness to responsibility. Developing responsibility is a natural process of maturation. Spiritual growth creates an inner willingness to change what you can to make the world a better place to live. Spiritual growth is closely linked to duty. It moves you from the cult of personality to the practice of principles.

(Self-)Absorbing Responsibility

You might be wondering, aren't there a lot of people with this flaw who take on excessive responsibility? Actually that is true. The roles that the self-absorbed play sometimes involve becoming heads of state, with global implications. I am sure you can name at least one. Let me suggest that our not so beloved Saddam Hussein is the best example of this flaw at the present time. He has so much wrong with his character that it is easy to pick on him. He took responsibility as part of a grab for power. Don't be lulled into thinking that because a person has offered to take care of you that he or she is selfless. Expecting to be taken care of could be destructive when you could take care of yourself.

The needs of others should become more important to you as you grow and mature, not the other way around. The self-absorbed see others as fulfilling their own needs. You have to be able to take care of yourself before you can take care of others. A mother has to find a way to save herself from the burning building in order to save the child. But self-regard run riot is not about taking good care of yourself. It is more likely associated with giving in to sensual gratification even when it would be dangerous or destructive. It is about seeing yourself as special by diminishing the importance of others. It is about maintaining infantile, selfish attitudes with everyone. It is about having things and using people, rather than having relationships and using things.

I Have a Right to Use These Defects in Character

You see this belief all the time. One of our working definitions of selfishness back in the office was "using a character flaw to one's advantage." Self-regard run riot then becomes a sort of solution to life's problems. At least it deludes you into believing that it is.

Extreme self-regard demands more rights than a person deserves. Actually a person has very few inalienable rights. Don't tell that to someone who is self-absorbed, or he or she will get very "annoyed" with you. IR³'s believe they have the right to use whatever character flaws benefit them, whenever they want. Selfishness is an attitude that allows the expression of all the other character flaws. Just as intolerance may connect the defects and enable a person to use them more easily, self-regard run riot is a facilitating flaw. In that sense, it is one of the more important flaws to get a handle on because it is a trigger for many other problems.

Aren't I Just Dazzling, Darling!

Here is how they try to dazzle you:

- They will walk all over people and explain how good it was for them
- They will flip from extremely self-important to victimized and back
- They will choke on envy and smile all the while
- They will show you that selfishness is not a problem but a sign of moral superiority
- They will show you that stealing is okay as long as they are doing it
- They will dazzle you with good intentions
- They will dazzle you with their inadequacies

They walk all over people and explain how good it was for them. I was visiting some friends a few years ago and one of them, Mack, had a large business that involved personal growth. He managed it with an iron fist. He wrapped it in a velvet glove, but it was an iron fist nevertheless. I was at the establishment reviewing some of his promotional materials. Mack called me into his office. He was excited because he was going to fire someone. "Lou, there is a real art to firing a person who is no longer good for the organization. You have to make them come away from the ordeal with the belief that you have just done them a favor. If you can do that, you help them and yourself. They will be able to find a new job faster and you will part as friends."

> **The infinitely little have a pride infinitely great.**
> **—VOLTAIRE**

I thought it was one of the wisest things I had ever heard. Later I found out that he'd had an affair with the lady. He was dumping her from work and terminating the relationship because she was no longer useful to him. I was lulled into believing he did it for her best interest. His game was pretending that he was really helping the unfortunate people who worked with him. My advice is to avoid people who beat you up for your own good.

They flip from extremely self-important to victimized and back. The self-absorbed who play victims in therapy often get told that they should take better care of themselves. That sounds reasonable on face value. What happens is that they flip-flop and become selfish rather than self-reliant. Often they have no idea what it means to be self-assured and think that they need to be self-centered. They immediately start to fix everyone else and punish anyone who has harmed them with a vengeance that would make an SS trooper jealous. I have heard therapists say to patients, "You need to be a little more selfish." The intention was good because they were talking to individuals who were whining and moaning about how self-sacrificing they were. More often than not the patients became selfish and vengeful in an effort to make their victimizer suffer. They were blind to their own self-will and distorted self-regard.

The other scenario that is fairly common occurs right after a person gets into recovery. Suddenly everyone else is an addict or alcoholic and the person starts to preach to his or her entire family. It happens with other diseases too. When people are diagnosed with an illness, especially cancer, they sometimes suddenly become experts and start preaching to everyone else about it, whether their audience wants to hear it or not. Mind you that is not as bad as victims becoming victimizers because they have been given permission to be selfish by their therapists.

All character readjustment should have the middle road of balance as a goal. Unfortunately people think that their insight into problems makes them experts. With this expert status they start to use this new character flaw to control others.

They choke on envy and smile while they are choking so you won't notice. Unless you can feel gratitude when someone else wins in life, your self-regard is out of control. That's a difficult thought to swallow, but envy is like that. If your self-regard has run riot on you, then you are constantly going to find yourself choking on envy, jealousy, and covetousness. You want to be the one who is more, has more, and does more. You are one of those who believe in the "mores." Not mores as in morality, but mores as in the plural of more and more. I could be happy if I had more, because I deserve more and more is better. Therefore let me use my character flaws to get more. When I get it, all I have is more stuff and less character. That's a plan that will eventually bring you to your knees. My advice is to get on your knees first and pray that you don't adopt that strategy. You will choke on your envy. There isn't a Heimlich maneuver that can free you either.

> There was one who thought himself above me, and he was above me until he had that thought.
> —ELBERT HUBBARD

They show you that selfishness is not a problem but a sign of moral superiority. What they pretend is that their brand of morality is superior to yours. "It is such a burden being so perfect." I can't begin to tell you who said that, because you might recognize him. He held public office and was confiding in me the way people often do when they hear that I am a psychiatrist. It sometimes is a burden, like when I am on an airplane for a flight next to a lady who wants me to cure her son by the time we land.

Self-absorbed people often do believe that they are perfect. This is especially true when they are riding high on the crest of a wave of success. The character flaw takes success to mean that it has come about because of moral superiority. That's a common flaw that often gets cured in the next round of adversity.

You probably want to know what my response was to Mr. Perfect above. "With all your humility," I said, "you won't find it a burden being perfect. It will just come naturally, like defecation."

Self-regard runs riot and then dazzles you with its obvious superiority. If it doesn't dazzle you, rest assured, it dazzles itself. Reality then beats it back to its senses. Most of the time these dazzling savants of modern morality believe that selfishness is only a minor problem when they have it. It is huge and needs immediate correction, though, when you have it. Now I bet you can think of a few self-absorbed people, can't you?

Your lust is always worse than my lust. Your gluttony is worse than my gluttony and your laziness is worse than mine.

I was on the beach with a couple of friends from medical school. We were reminiscing about the good ol' times and talking about relationships. One of the guys gave a nice lecture to the other about lust and sexual fantasies. He said, "You shouldn't even think about other women. The Bible says that if you lust after her in your heart it is the same as adultery." Meanwhile, which one was having the affair? That's right, the preacher.

Somehow this character flaw must increase intuition. It seems like it is the selfish who know just what issues to pick on to hurt you. They are uncanny. Often they will set you up so that you can't possibly confront them back, because they have played the game of being humble. Before they point out the errors of your way they admit that they were scoundrels. "Listen, you know I'm not a saint, and I've got my faults . . ." That way they can't be held accountable because they've already denied having any moral standards, but they are still superior to you.

They show you that stealing is okay as long as they are doing it. I call this the Robin Hood syndrome. Self-absorbed people know that they have a right to your possessions. You aren't capable of using them as wisely as they are, so it is just fine if they relieve you of them. Sounds like the tax collector to me. It isn't that they are stealing, they are just putting the stuff that's out there to better use than you would. They know.

Actually, where I come from taking someone else's things for whatever reason is still stealing. It is dishonest to make elaborate justifications for immoral actions, but when self-regard runs riot the justifications really do seem believable. IR³'s have selfish motives for their dishonesty. They may try to convince you that their motives are high and come from the almighty, but they are just high and mighty. A reform, no matter how well intentioned, that reforms other people and not oneself is really not a reformation but a coercion. The self-absorbed are naturally addicted to being right and they are naturally quick to blame. They use the other character flaws because they have a right to. They lie and cheat because they have your best interest at stake. The bottom line is that stealing is okay because they are doing it.

A young man came to my office with a simple anxiety disorder. It was nothing too complicated. In the course of treatment he revealed that he was a burglar by hobby. "I only steal from those I think can afford it."

"Why you're a veritable Robin Hood, aren't you?" I said.

"You bet, Doc. And don't worry, I don't plan on hitting your office."

They dazzle you with good intentions. He wanted me to feel grateful for his benevolence. His self-importance was interpreted by his ego as kindness. I politely thanked him for the favor and then asked him to get a book on Robin Hood so we could discuss the principles involved.

One more thing sick self-regard will do is to pretend stupidity. **They will dazzle you with their inadequacies**. This final ploy is a method to get you to commit to something that leaves you vulnerable. When a person has self-regard running riot and comes to you with "I don't really understand" or "I am not smart like you," watch out. They are getting ready to launch an attack. They are raging indignants or the addicted to being right setting you up.

Debbie, a legal assistant, came to my office to work on relationship problems. She was constantly arguing with her husband, who was a physician. "Doc, look, I don't have your expertise in these matters," she would say. "Let me ask you something, just your opinion."

It was like sitting in a deposition with a really slick lawyer. At first I fell into the trap of being flattered that she wanted a bit of my great wisdom. It didn't take me too long to figure out that she wasn't trying to inform herself of my opinion. She was setting me up to prove that as dense as she was, she was superior to her husband. I was dazzled for a bit. I referred the couple to a therapist who reported back to me that they both played that game. They were both addicted to being right. He was a raging indignant and she was a helpless victim.

The Convictions of Conceit

Your self-aggrandized neighbors who are staring into the pool of life with Narcissus have deep spiritual problems. They have the seven beliefs listed below, that don't work, but their egos are running rampant trying to force these beliefs. See if you recognize them in yourself. We are all taught them, but as we mature we recognize that they are not entirely true. Remember that we mature from selfishness to selflessness and let go of these convictions of conceit along the way.

- I can't compete and get more
- More is better
- Life won't provide enough for me
- Money or "stuff" will solve the problem
- Letting go is dangerous
- God isn't going to take care of us
- If God can't, fame will

I can't compete and get more. This is the start of a whole cycle of problems with the self-regard running riot. They believe that if they do compete they might lose. That is reasonable, since there is no guaranteed winning in life. They are not, however, in the game to lose, only to win. It's not a game either. Their self-esteem has been hurt in the past by failure and now they need to control how they feel. They suffer from wounded pride and are going to compensate. It was Archbishop Fulton J. Sheen who pointed out, "Pride is an admission of weakness; it secretly fears all competition and dreads all rivals." They feel weak, powerless or feeble and can't stand it so they overcompensate.

The first part of the overcompensation is to develop the next stage of belief, **more is better**. I have already explained how that works. You could be happy if you had more, and you deserve more. More is the answer. Let me add here that "more is better" applies to your ego too. Self-regard running riot requires a bloated ego. More stuff, more money, more respect, more children, more of anything you lack will fill the hole in your soul. Ego is perceived as the great soul filler. It is a never-ending quest.

It leaves you with the feeling that you must reach for more. You are sadly not like the birds of the field, for whom God, through nature, will provide. This is different from "I can't compete." There is a dread that **"life won't provide enough for me**, regardless of how hard I work." Often these self-absorbed people have seen their role models struggle through adversity and fail. They have experienced periods of trauma and believe along with everyone else that **money or stuff will solve the problem**. It is such a disappointment when it fails. A young and very successful broker came to my office after caving in emotionally. He had hit all his goals and still felt inadequate. He had the fancy car, the beautiful palace in an exclusive suburb, the respect of older colleagues on "The Street." He still felt empty inside. He had filled the hole in his soul with money, possessions, respect from others, a wife, and soon a child. He was still lost. It was like a black hole sucking in everything and compressing it to nothing.

The real crisis he faced was how he could be a good father and still compete full-tilt on "The Street." There was barely enough time for his wife. He was married to his cell phone and his clients. The idea of taking responsibility for a new and precious life was driving him to examine what was important. He also knew that he had much less control over his life with a child. He resented that. At some point he faced a problem that many of us must confront. **Letting go is dangerous**.

Letting go of our attachments to things or even to people can be very liberating. For those suffering through life at the hands of this character flaw it is terrifying. Often mature individuals make peace with their creator. They come to believe that God will provide. They even learn to face tough times, exhausting every possibility knowing full well that miracles don't occur until all your "normal" avenues are exhausted. Individuals with this flaw are still chanting I, me, mine with the Beatles, hoping to overcome their problems. They don't believe in miracles. They secretly know that **God isn't going to take care of us**.

If I won't let God, because God can't, then I must find some new magical power to turn my life into the miracle it should be. What is the greatest miracle to a Texas-sized ego looking for fulfillment from the world? You guessed it, "fame!" The last conviction of conceit is, **"If God can't, fame will."** Self-regard run riot discovers a great truth. It can run riot better with a little bit of fame, or a little bit more, than it can with humility and surrender. When fame becomes your obsession, you can kiss character good-bye. Fame celebrates uniqueness. Egos revel in fame. The self-absorbed seek their place in history, not by serving mankind but by trying to make "history."

Great fame is elusive to most who pursue it. Yet often the price of its pursuit is the sacrifice of virtue. If you don't believe me go ask all the great dead movie stars, singers, and other entertainers who lost their lives to drugs and alcohol pursuing the dream created by this character flaw. Did I just write dream? I meant nightmare. You see, the way it really is was best stated by Oliver Wendell Holmes. He said, "Fame usually comes to those who are thinking about something else." Fame for fame's sake is a nightmare.

Those who die for fame die for an illusion. There is no pride in dying for an illusion. Great fame without character is an illusion. It is false pride, taken to infamy. What good is it to be well known for being a scoundrel? Would you teach your children to pursue fame and go the path of a Jeffrey Dahmer, the serial murderer? Of course not. Yet our culture glorifies personality, not principles of character.

While I was taking a course in forensic psychiatry, the evaluation and treatment of criminals with mental illness, my professor pointed out that he had evaluated a murderer who studied how other murderers killed. This human monster wanted to be famous.

Self-regard run riot drives the soul to seek the rewards of vanity. They turn out to be sparse, and often quite unfullfilling. In fact more often than not false pride ends up creating disgrace by sacrificing one's values to get ahead. It is just that the disgrace is more well known than if it had been someone less famous.

America's foremost expert on character transformation, Benjamin Franklin, put it this way, "Pride breakfasted with Plenty, dined with Poverty, supped with Infamy." If you want evidence Franklin was right, watch any famous public figure who you sense is embellishing his or her own virtue. Look to see if some of the other character flaws are there and then be patient. Wait a few years. He or she will eventually sup with infamy.

Self-regard run riot feeds on fame. It feeds on that moment in time when all eyes are turned upon its ugly narcissistic face. It feeds on self-importance, puffing people up till they almost explode with grandiosity. It is difficult to manage, though. It is like eating Jell-O while riding a roller coaster. If your fame is not unsought, if it is not based on pristine character and selfless service, it will be a meal that is difficult to eat without getting you and the rest of us sick.

You Are Expendable!

This is a crucial point because it is a belief that both the humble and proud hold dear. The difference is quite simple. Self-aggrandizing people believe that *you* are expendable and will use you for whatever they are trying to accomplish. The humble see themselves as expendable and are willing to sacrifice themselves for the overall good of mankind.

The self-absorbed feel that they are missing something indispensable and want to be that something for everyone else. Their secret hope is to become a sort of drug for others to depend on. The humble servants of humanity see that each of us is that something indispensable. They see that nothing is missing as long as they serve everyone else and express that something special as love.

One comes away with an ego desperately hoping to be needed for its uniqueness. The other goes out to give so that he or she can be of service to you and me. One faces the world with core issues of grandiosity/inadequacy, empty of real meaning. The other sees meaning everywhere. Which one are you?

Married to Narcissus

We use the myth of Narcissus to explain personalities that are like that poor fellow stuck looking at his beautiful reflection in the pool. Did you notice who he marries?

No one.

That's right. No one comes to the pool and then no one agrees that he is beautiful and of course no one wants to spend the rest of her life with him.

> That man who lives for self alone,
> Lives for the meanest mortal known.
> —JOAQUIN MILLER

You are never going to find a person who can stay married to someone who has self-regard run riot. You may find that the self-absorbed have a lot of relationships, especially with those who are victims or who believe that they are inadequate. You may find self-regard running riot in bizarre jobs, like the exotic dancers who often came in for therapy because of their sick relationships. Desiree, a well-known dancer who used another stage name, came in to complain about her boyfriend. "He's not bothered by the exotic dancing that I do, or the erotic private shows. He is very understanding, doctor, but now he wants to settle down and marry me."

I knew her boyfriend had to be odd, just based on that one statement. He was a rescuer trying to salvage a life that was quickly going down the tubes with an array of addictive substances and illegal activities.

As long as he worshiped her, she was fine. As soon as he wanted a more boring (read that as normal) relationship, she came in looking for help. She wanted a psychiatrist to help her dump her boyfriend.

Ego Deflation and Marital Elation!

No other character flaw has quite the effect on the ego that this one does. There should be a diagnosis called swollen ego syndrome or inflammation of the ego, "egoitis." A large ego is a death knell to a marriage. If the two coming into a marriage cannot see the relationship as more important than their own egos, the marriage is doomed. A swollen ego keeps a man or woman from being humble. Humility is almost as important as love in maintaining a marriage. It is no wonder that swollen egos don't function well in marriages.

I really do believe that God instituted the bond of Holy Matrimony as an instrument to reduce your ego. Marriage is a kind of salve. When it is applied with enough love each of the partners gets to eat the wedding cake of humble pie. This essentially causes a rapid decrease in self-regard run riot. It is simultaneously associated with a dramatic increase in spirituality accompanied with hearing God's name from your partner. Most often it sounds like, "Oh God, how did I wind up with this idiot?"

God responds by letting you understand that the true nature of a spiritual union is that your partner reflects or complements your character flaws. It's a humbling experience. The self-absorbed can't do it. The humility is too painful. The love is not deep enough to tolerate it.

Self-regard run riot causes the individual to see the spouse as an appendage. The wife is not a partner but a piece of the marriage deal the man got into. He can change wives relatively simply. There was never a marriage in a sacred sense because life, at least the other person's, wasn't sacred. This pattern is associated with people who chronically feel something is missing in life. The other person is supposed to complete them. When that fails, as it always does, the marriage is over.

Some people never grow up. They manage to maintain the child-ish immaturity of this character flaw. The self-regard of a five-year-old will never work in a marriage. Some of you reading this book know from personal experience what I mean.

The Illusion of Success

Little kids often make decisions that are based on greed. It's okay for them to try and take a little more. It is fairly normal. We teach them to share so that they can fit in and function. They will learn self-sacrifice when they raise their own children later on.

When adults, however, try selfishness at work, they often quickly advance. They think that they have found the solution to success. This is only an illusion of success. True success comes from provid-ing a service, not from selfishness. Grabbing power isn't success. It is depotism. Being an authority requires knowledge, not the power to keep everything revolving around you. Vanity is not a requirement of leadership.

Interrupting Narcissus at the Pond

So what do you do if you are with the self-absorbed? How do you deal with them and maintain your sanity? It can be difficult because even something as innocuous as walking into a room creates a desire to be the center of attention.

- Point out when they need to be more of a team player
- Privately confront their desire to control
- Ask them to share responsibilities
- Ask them to give recognition to others
- Focus on their virtues and values over their status
- Be respectfully direct

The self-absorbed want to win even if it means hogging the ball. **Point out when they need to be more of a team player**. It may be difficult for them to participate on a team without having control or directing everything, but it is important to make sure you keep them a part of the team. When they are not the team leader, make sure that you acknowledge the person who has that role. In group therapy, the self-absorbed seemed to always try to run the group. We would acknowledge the role of the co-therapist so that the patient would be forced to be part of and not lead the group.

Privately confront their desire to control. When people who have self-regard run riot get emotionally involved in any project their desire to control takes over. I'm sure there are good intentions behind it, but it is disruptive. Since they have such fragile egos, it is often better to confront them privately. "I know you really want this project to work, and I respect your willingness to help, but you need to tone down . . ." Describe the behavior that needs to be changed.

Ask them to share responsibilities. Sometimes it is like working with an adolescent. Share your toys becomes share your ideas and share other people's ideas too. When they start to see that they are empowered by the relationships they have with others they are easier to deal with.

Ask them to give recognition to others. This has an amazing effect on the self-absorbed. I made one of my medical students responsible for putting together an evaluation of his peers. He had to create a mechanism that would effectively demonstrate what the other students' strengths were. It was my way of getting him involved in recognizing others. I was also trying to channel his desire to control.

Focus on their virtues and values over their status. Point out the moral and ethical victories that the self-absorbed make. Since most of their decisions revolve around self-aggrandizement and not self-esteem, you can help them by focusing on their values when they make the "tough decision." In my practice we used to ask, "So, are you going to do the right thing?"

Be respectfully direct. Peggy Messina, the addictions counselor in my office, used to say, "So, did God die and leave you in charge?" I still can't figure out how she used to say that and get away with it, but she did, because patients knew that she was only confronting their behavior. She held her patients in high esteem. Be direct, but be respectful.

Vanity Fears Laughter

The simplest cure for your own vanity, if it has become a character flaw, is to laugh at yourself. Since I am going to assume that you are far too serious a person to do that, let me give you some other suggestions.

- Treat everyone as your equal
- Be alike to everyone—no airs
- Turn selfishness into service
- Accept responsibility with humility
- Practice positive values
- Be invisible whenever possible
- Go teach some children how to share
- Be the wind beneath someone else's wings

Treat everyone as your equal. They are anyhow, so you may as well get used to reality. Why resist it? A patient came in after an experience of "spiritual oneness with the universe" and said to me, "Everyone is my equal. No one is less, none is better, we are one." Her mystical experience was the exact opposite of this character flaw.

Be alike to everyone—no airs. Talk about an easy solution to inflammation of the ego. This is it! If you or any self-absorbed person that you know could just be alike to everyone for twenty-four hours you would see a remarkable transformation. Most of us have our little roles that we play all day long. For instance I am a husband to my wife and a father to my children. Other professionals see me as a psychiatrist, and still others as their friend. All day long, though, I try just to let myself be consistently me. It used to get me in trouble, but now it gets me involved in a lot of other people's lives because I am a gift to them. Often they believe otherwise.

Turn selfishness into service. The more you become involved in being of service to others, the faster self-regard run riot will leave your character. It is a known fact that service is very high on the ladder of spirituality. It is tremendously rewarding to choose voluntarily to help others with no expectation of reward. That is the foundation for this principle, but I am also referring to business dealings and relationships where there are many rewards. Look to see what role you play in being of service to others. You will find the rewards come back to you many times over. Another thing will happen. That secret desire for more responsibility that everyone with this flaw has is fulfilled.

Accept responsibility with humility. It is one thing to accept more responsibility and another to accept it with greater humility. This is exactly what is necessary in order to keep from increasing the grip this character flaw has upon you. Every time you gain a rung on the ladder of success or fame, you risk getting more involved in selfishness. Care has to be taken not to become more grandiose. Christ washed the feet of the disciples to teach them this principle when

He instituted the priesthood. Gandhi cleaned toilets when the British complained. Responsibility demands greater humility. You are being asked to serve more people when more responsibility is given you. The average IR³ thinks it means he or she is getting recognition. That means you get to accept more stress.

Practice positive values. There are a few very key points here. Keep a positive attitude toward others. Read positive literature. Associate with positive people. And practice values that will make you a better servant to others. This also means avoiding negative people. These are the self-aggrandizing, ego-inflamed darlings of the world who usually practice one or more of these flaws. Practicing positive values means deciding that you will consciously shift from the belief that you have to take as much as you can. Shift to a new belief that you have to give back as much as you can. Carnegie did it and Rockefeller tried it with a little less success. Carnegie funded the great public library system in the United States. He gave away all of his money. In today's currency it would probably be worth $250 billion!

Be a team player. Don't just try to get others to be team players. Be the example. People with this flaw are notoriously selfish and want to be the star. Learn to be a team player first and let your unique talents lift everyone.

Be invisible whenever possible. This is really a stretch for the average IR³. Most of us cherish being the center of attention. We love when the event is centered around us. We love the recognition and acknowledgments. We crave the fame. At least we do if this flaw has us in its clutches.

It was William Penn who said, "Do what good thou canst unknown, and be not vain of what ought rather to be felt than seen." Do something anonymous for a change. I don't mean be someone's anonymous father. Go offer your service to someone and ask them not to speak to anyone about the fact that you helped out. Share a random act of kindness. I used to pay the toll for the car behind me at the Verrazano Narrows Bridge. I was single at the time and thought it was a cheap way to meet young ladies. I stopped when they raised the price on the bridge. That's not what I mean by doing something anonymously.

I have a friend, who will stay anonymous in this book, who gives half of his gross income to charity. He makes many millions of dollars a year, yet he gives it away. He loves to give. He needs to give. In spite of giving half of everything he makes away, he gets richer every year.

When I first went into practice I had a young patient who was dying of kidney failure. He was a child diabetic who as a young man had finally come to the end stage of his disease. He had a young wife and a little boy. As a father he couldn't provide for his family. They could barely make ends meet. At Christmastime an anonymous donor, through some private foundation, sent them a check that allowed the family to celebrate with a tree and presents. This anonymous act of kindness was a miracle in their lives. But more than that, it touched the heart of everyone in my office. I am sure that wherever they told that story someone was uplifted. Whoever did it has chosen to remain anonymous. That's practicing the opposite of this character flaw.

I look at people who go on TV to disclose that they have given away a bazillion dollars to the poor. They have discovered charity as another means of self-aggrandizement. I felt sorry that Mrs. Kroc

> The charity that hastens to proclaim its good deeds ceases to be charity, and is only pride and ostentation.
> —WILLIAM HUTTON

was discovered to be the anonymous donor to the South Dakota flood victims. She had given millions of dollars away to these unfortunate people who had lost everything. I didn't see revealing her identity as investigative journalism as much as flawed characters trying rob someone of great spiritual benefit.

If you want to practice selfless service go teach some children how to share. It is a tedious process. Little children are usually naturally greedy with moments of generosity. Trying to teach them this process helps us understand how childish we are when we are filled with desires.

Fly Higher Than an Eagle!

We have all been inspired by someone who has served to be the wind beneath our wings. We have been lifted up by great example. We have been inspired by true dedication to high ideals. Many of you have had the opportunity to be mentored by the leaders in your chosen career. I am grateful to the many teachers who have deliberately chosen not to practice this flaw so that they could be of greater benefit to mankind. They have been an inspiration to me.

I remember a young professor of biology, Joseph Gennaro, who inspired me to study, and to achieve. He was always available for students who showed a love of his subject. He was even available after graduation as a friend and mentor.

I have had the marvelous opportunity to study with great teachers. There have been professors of medicine, surgery, and psychiatry who have worked diligently with me. These doctors dedicated themselves to the care of patients. One of their vehicles for enhancing patient care was to train others. Their goal was to bring out the best in me so that I could be of some use to my patients. Even those with gigantic egos, when teaching, were really quite selfless. My gratitude is undying. They taught first of all that the true teachers are our patients. Everything we will ever need to know will come directly or indirectly from our patients.

The well-being of those patients was far more important than their egos. It was remarkable to see the sacrifice and dedication they displayed. It certainly is very different than what is portrayed on the hospital melodramas.

What we do when we are mentored is to adopt the other person's view or beliefs about life and our profession. I call that the high-altitude view. It is a high-altitude view when your mentor is person of character. It is a high-altitude view when you adopt the values that have driven your mentor. Get that high-altitude view and fly higher than an eagle.

Great mentors share very common beliefs. First of all they give away their knowledge to help make the world a better place for everyone else.

Second, they are down-to-earth enough to see the world from your point of view. Try that with other people and you will immediately be forced to let go of the flaw. My greatest mentors saw all three sides to the coin. My side, their side, and the truth.

It is simple to test for selfishness, it just isn't done very often. When you shift your view of a problem or situation to the other person's point of view you have to let go of selfishness. In group we occasionally had people switch chairs and role-play being the person they were jealous of.

Great mentors give recognition and accept responsibility. Watch the great football coaches talk about the men who won the game. Then watch when there is a loss. They take responsibility for the defeat. They give recognition and accept responsibility. If giving recognition becomes more important than taking credit, you are definitely on your way to releasing this flaw.

The people in your world are an expression of life to you. They are a gift from the creator, to teach you the lessons you need to learn. Participate in their lives. Participate selflessly. Celebrate others. Celebrate their joys. Share their sorrows. Bring to them the best you that you can be. When you start giving yourself away to everyone without expectation of respect, gratitude, or recognition, something dramatic happens. The holes in your soul that were driving you to seek fame, vanity, and respect from others will be filled. They will be filled to overflowing, no longer holes but wellsprings of life's creative energy flowing through you for the benefit of humanity.

The choice is yours. Celebrate others and realize that your cup is overflowing or use the next character flaw, inadequacy, and have an excuse for everything. I think you know what choice to make.

The Excuse for Everything— Inadequacy

HOW DO YOU KNOW IF YOU HAVE *THE EXCUSE FOR EVERYTHING—INADEQUACY?*

1. Do you hide your inadequacy with pomposity and like it?

2. Do you love your own excuses because you invented them?

3. Do you quit before you have given it your all?

4. Do you believe that you were born to the wrong race, parents, or society?

5. Do you believe that you can't because you weren't raised properly?

6. Do you use inadequacy so that you can justify having other character flaws?

7. When you look at your own life, do you get filled with pity?

8. Do you claim incompetence when you get in trouble?

9. Do you believe that you were given a defective body?

10. Do you believe that you weren't given a good enough mind?

11. Do you believe that it is too difficult to develop new abilities?

12. Do you believe that being inadequate relieves you of responsibility?

13. When other people lose, do you feel a little more normal?

14. When you have a party is it a "pity party"?

15. Do you find yourself investing more time in excuses than doing?

16. Do you accept "try" rather than "do"?

17. Do you dislike competition?

18. Do you use other people's inadequacies as an excuse?

19. Do you refuse to look and develop your potential?

A stooped over, gray-haired set designer for Federico Fellini was in my office being treated for depression. Franco, as I will call him in this story, was worn out by the tumultuous life he had lived and was now nearly destitute in a single-room occupancy, or SRO, in New York. Most of the reasons for his demise, he said, were not in his control. His biggest excuse, though, was that he could never make it again in *Cinema Città,* or the Italian version of Hollywood, because he was too old and infirm. He was inadequate.

He still had control over his ability to pray, though.

During the course of a session he noticed the autographed photo of Mother Teresa on my wall and confessed his loss of faith. Franco never prayed anymore. In this situation people pray for miracles that they don't believe in so that they can keep their faith in God buried beneath a pile of bitter disappointments. I suspected that he did too. Since he was having a bout with cancer, I knew it was time for him to rekindle some spirituality.

"I lost my relationship with God years ago, *Dottore*," he said. "It would take a small miracle for me to get it back." He hung his head in shame.

I figured that if he was supposed to get his faith back he was due for a miracle, but he didn't even believe he was capable of praying. I asked him to pray with me. "Ask for something big and definitely something you couldn't possibly do on your own. There is no such thing as a big or little miracle for God. Let's go for something grand." Fortunately he took my challenge. He knew exactly what to ask for. He picked something that he believed couldn't happen in a thousand years. He prayed that someone from *Cinema Città* would ask him to go to work. That would be unheard of. He hadn't been in touch with anyone in the industry for nearly a decade. Hollywood types don't normally have a long memory when someone fails.

"If that happened would your faith come back?" I asked.

"*Si, Dottore*. And I would stop making excuses."

I had one simple demand. "Franco, stop praying for it. You asked once. That's enough. Just promise me that whenever you think about it you will remind yourself that the crazy *Dottore* believes it with his whole heart. Don't you pray for it anymore. You could ruin it." He thought I was one of the most peculiar people he had ever met.

A few days later he burst into my office, hair dyed back to brown, wearing a new sport coat and an ascot. He looked dashing and at least fifteen years younger.

"You won't believe it. An old friend tracked me down and I am going out west to build a set for a new spaghetti western."

It eventually became one the most popular shows on TV in Europe. His set was used for a number of westerns.

So much for his alleged inadequacy.

Giving Birth to Excuses

Excuses are terribly difficult to give up. In order to understand why, you have to understand how we make them and use them. You and I create reasons that explain reality. Like most of our creative thoughts we find them fascinating. At first we do it simply to have some meaning. Often they explain why things don't work. That is in and of itself very useful.

We are apt to defend our excuses, since they are the children of our creativity. We defend them like we would any bright idea. We defend them like we would our own children. If you don't believe me, try this. Instead of arguing with others over their stupid excuses, ask them for all the reasons why they are good excuses. Then

> **An excuse is worse and more terrible than a lie; for an excuse is a lie guarded.**
> **—ALEXANDER POPE**

watch what happens. Average mortals will ramble on about what a wonderful idea the obviously stupid excuses are. They will hunt for justifications for their lovely excuses. Hey, once you've given birth to the baby, you have to take care of it.

If you have found an excuse that has worked in the past, it is more likely that you will use it in the future. It's like a good tool. It makes the job easier.

Inadequacy: The Universal Donor of Excuses

Suppose you found an excuse that worked nearly all the time and could be used on anyone, without suffering great rejection. Wouldn't that be useful? You could pick and choose what you did, and how you did it. When you didn't keep your word or live up to expectations you would have the great justification. You could take the excuse out of your box of emotional tools and use it in various areas of your life.

Suppose you could find an excuse that mobilized people to help you, created self-pity, allowed you to use your favorite character flaws whenever you liked. That would be a great excuse, wouldn't it?

Suppose it allowed you to reveal whether people loved you or not. How about if it could be used to get people off your back? Wouldn't it just be terrific?

Well, there is an excuse for everything. It is called inadequacy. The only price you have to pay for it is your self-esteem. If you don't have high self-esteem, being inadequate could be purchased at a bargain price.

Rocky and Gideon

Two of my favorite heroes, one fantasy, one biblical, are lessons in this character flaw. You all know Rocky Balboa's story. He had to pay a steep price because he chose to use inadequacy as his excuse. He never really meant his life to be as bad as it was. He was cutting himself a little slack by agreeing with those around him who didn't believe. Life rarely offers you a chance to go against Apollo Creed. Usually it gives you an opponent who is just a little tougher than you believe yourself to be. Choose inadequacy and lose, or choose self-esteem and fight the fight of your life. You can't be knocked out if you absolutely refuse.

So how does inadequacy present itself? Take Gideon for instance. Here was a young man trying to hide some wheat in a winepress so that the Midionites wouldn't take it from him. The tribes of Israel were being oppressed by hundreds of thousands of men who roamed around the land taking everything they could. Poor Gideon gets confronted by an angel with a sense of humor. The very first thing the angel does is to call Gideon a champion, and tell him the Lord is with him.

Gideon may be inadequate, but he is no fool. He asks the angel the great question. That is: "If the Lord is with me, why?" We all ask that question. How come, God? Why does bad stuff happen to me?

Gideon gets the same answer the rest of us always get. "Go with the strength you have and save Israel." Go do something with what you have and make things better. That's the key. But Gideon has the great excuse. He tells the angel that he is inadequate. Well, actually he doesn't use those words. He offers substantial proof and is going to let the angel figure out that he is inadequate. He tells the angel that he is in the meanest family and he is the lowliest son. In other words, you've got the wrong guy, I am inadequate.

Of course, he raises an army and wipes out the enemy in such a short time that it has to be a miracle.

The point is that inadequacy is not acceptable in the eyes of God. So you are going to have to give it up. Before you do, though, you probably will need to know a little more about it. It is the key to unlocking high self-esteem and discovering untapped potential.

I Regret to Inform You, You Are Adequate!

Most of us have suffered from some self-pity. We have tried being lazy and felt guilt. If you haven't you are a sociopath and lying about yourself. So put this book down and go read a novel. We all develop the capacity for shame at about the same time we develop intact egos, about three to five years of age. There are some good and bad uses of all of these traits. Excess with any of them is a problem. This character flaw works like a shield. It holds out our feebleness or our shame as a weapon to keep people away so that we don't have to be tested. You may not like exams, but life is going to test you. There is no other way to discover who you are and what your capabilities are without being tested. Not trying may seem easier. Declaring "I am inadequate" may work for a while, but the seeds of greatness that are planted within your soul will germinate with or without your permission.

> **He that is good for making excuses is seldom good for anything else.**
> **—BENJAMIN FRANKLIN**

If you have been using excuses for not trying, if you have pretended to be incompetent, eventually regret starts. Something inside knows that you have to make do with what you have, and it is always enough. The regret for not doing all you are capable of will haunt you. No one can choose to be incompetent and feel good about it. Eventually the part of you that knows better gets outraged. It will start to cleave off the rough edges of the raw diamond that you are, with or without your permission. When that happens the character flaw starts to lose its power. Your soul wants to sparkle and it can't be denied.

Better Than the Man in the Glass

You might know that poem "The Man in the Glass." I won't repeat it here, but it's about how you can fool the whole world but you have to be accountable to yourself. It refers quite eloquently to the issue of comparison and self-acceptance. Self-esteem is highest in those of us who compare ourselves to others the least. What we are not taught is that we have to be careful about comparing ourselves to who we think we ought to be, to be self-accepting. We all have an image of how we are supposed to be. When we look in the mirror and see something different we are filled with guilt and shame. We feel inadequate. That is self-rejection. Or we get filled with the motivation to change, because we are self-accepting.

Did you ever wonder how that works? Most people don't. They feel the guilt and do very little about it. Here is what happens. We look at our internal image of who we should be. That's called our idealized self. Then we compare that idealized self to who we think we are. If there is a great difference we feel tense or guilty. Next we take the image and put it out into our future, until it feels right. Now our ideal is out there and it becomes a goal. So, simply stated, you think about what you should become, and then turn it into what you could become. If you are motivated, you will start the process of achieving the ideal. When you face the person in the glass you are faced with someone who is working on becoming better.

We run into problems when we have an idealized self that can never be achieved. That idealized self is too different from who we are or even think we could become. It causes us to be frustrated with ourselves. When we create an idealized self based upon comparison with others we can never feel adequate, or we always feel arrogant. Or worse yet we compare ourselves not with an idealized self but the idealized self that we believe others have. We compare ourselves and either come out short or come up long. It is either inadequacy or the flip side of the same phenomenon, arrogance.

Whenever we compare ourselves to our idealized selves we will feel either motivated or inactivated. If at the same time we compare ourselves to someone else, then we risk losing our self-esteem. We believe, "I am not enough." Normal people who aren't possessed by this flaw look at where they come up short and see it as reason for change. They have a healthy underlying belief about themselves.

What Must Others Think of Me

I was a teenager and worked on a committee for a high school computerized dance. It was in the days of punch cards and old IBM mainframes. We had hundreds of high school students fill out questionnaires about their personal preferences. Then we had printouts of who matched as dance partners based on similarities in answers. I must confess that the night before the dance I went in and manipulated the results. I was already a student of human behavior, curious to watch people's reactions. I wanted to see what would happen when the tallest guy had to dance with the shortest girl. When the smartest girl had to dance with the slowest football player, how would they react? On and on, we had dozens of pairs who were put together by me and one other person who shall remain nameless. I hope some of my classmates are reading this. It is a confession, and amends to you all.

During the dance I looked across the hall and saw one of the best-looking guys dancing with a very plain girl. He was being quite polite and very pleasant with her. She had always been very reserved and cautious. Suddenly she cut loose and danced with abandon. Something had happened to her perception of who she was.

At the same time I was worrying about what all the extremely pretty young ladies would be thinking of me. You guessed it. Of course I had loaded my list of dance partners with all the girls I secretly wanted to dance with. I was nervous and worried that I would be rejected. Then I realized that all the young ladies were just as worried about what I thought of them. I promised myself I would spend more time thinking about other people and stop worrying about what people thought of me. It was a liberating realization.

What You Are Is Not Who You Are!

I could write a whole book on this topic. Self with a capital "S" is much more than you can imagine. So often we shortchange ourselves into believing that we are what we are. But we are not. Do I have you confused yet? Good.

You are not your body, you have a body. You are not what you do. You are not your behavior, right? You are the observer of your deeds. You are not your thoughts. So you are not your mind either. You have a mind, at least I would think so because you are reading this.

You are not your feelings. You have your feelings and your sensations. You are the being who experiences these feelings and sensations. So bear with me just a little more. You are not your body or your thoughts. You are not your sensations or your feelings. Then who the heck are you? You are the still, silent "I am" that exists between the thoughts, observing all the activity.

Okay, so even if you do know that, how does it help? When you are comparing yourself to others, what are you comparing? Your thoughts, your behavior, your physical presence? What is it that you compare? Is it the part of you that is transient, or is it the eternal you?

All inadequacy comes from not understanding this point. You are not your body, or your mind. You are the being, awareness, and love that observes the body and mind. When you make pictures of your idealized self it is always about the body or about the mind. You have been duped into believing that you are a mind with a body, or worse yet a body with a mind. You are pure spiritual essence with the experience of a body and mind.

When you fail to realize that you are being, awareness, and love and you overidentify with your body or mind, then you risk feeling unloved. That starts a whole series of problems such as not being self-forgiving, feeling like you have no power or too little ability. Basically you start to come up short and experience inadequacy.

Trying to be a body rather than have one is a universal conflict. It haunts anyone with any degree of ambition. The fact that the issue is rarely ever addressed doesn't make it go away. Ask your average college graduate if he or she is a body or a mind or both or something beyond both. That will get you a lot of strange looks.

Try asking people if they have ever had any feelings of inadequacy related to the size, shape, and look of their body and you will get a universal yes. Ask if they have ever felt inadequate due to the abilities of their mind and you will almost always get a yes.

By being a body-mind rather than a spiritual being with a body-mind we come away with a feeling of not being good enough. Sometimes it is just a fleeting feeling. For inadequate people, feeling unloved and unworthy of love is a lifetime experience. To feel loved and appreciated, people with deep inadequacies will do almost anything. They may lie, cheat, or cover up for other people. Inadequate people will try living other people's morals, sacrificing their own just to feel that they look good in the eyes of others. Even worse, some people pay for their need to be loved and appreciated with sex. Sex becomes equated with love, or as they say, an erection means affection. You know the outcome. Sexual encounters before a committed relationship has had a chance to form are a hallmark of this flaw. There is nothing sacred in their sexuality. Inadequacy grows because the act is degraded.

When inadequacy becomes the excuse that is at the bottom of all the other excuses the obvious outcome is the inability to do anything well. We now have the excuse for laziness, inactivity, and failure at anything. As Nathaniel Howe said, "The way to be nothing is to do nothing." Prolonged idleness causes a further decrease in ability and kills initiative. It is a downward cycle. It ends up with a lose-lose strategy for life.

Lose-Lose Strategy

This is a way of dealing with situations that leaves all parties worse off but protects the rights of everyone to be inadequate. That may not sound like a strategy that anyone you know has ever employed. You are used to people facing life's journey with a win-win strategy.

HERE IS WHAT THE LOSE-LOSE STRATEGY CONSISTS OF:

- I don't have the abilities
- It is too difficult to develop them
- I am not responsible
- I am in the wrong place
- I feel bad that I will lose
- I want you to feel bad with me
- If you lose too I won't feel so bad
- Let's lower standards and call failure a win for everybody

First the inadequate acknowledges that he or she doesn't have the necessary abilities. A normal person would try to develop them but the character flaw of inadequacy leads one to believe that it isn't worth working on. It is usually because it seems too difficult. That isn't the real issue. What is actually going on is that the abilities don't seem worth the struggle to develop them. When children are not doing well in math or reading they have to believe that it is important to learn these things even if they come slowly. If it is not of value they won't bother.

My friend Les Brown was dyslexic. Reading was terribly difficult for him as a child. Yet today he is an avid reader and now an author too. He knew the ability was worth the struggle. Losers don't believe that. The character flaw says to give up even before you try.

Next you get confronted with the belief that you are not responsible for the ability. If you are not capable of doing something it is a complete waste of time blaming anyone for it. You either decide to get the capability or decide not to. But the lose-lose strategy demands that you fix the blame on someone else. If there is no one else, then at least you can assure everyone that you are not responsible.

There is another slightly distorted belief that kicks in with this strategy. It is the belief that somehow the universe has messed up and you are in the wrong place at the right time. Again this helps relieve you of the responsibility. Let's not make anyone responsible, that way you can affirm that you are powerless, or at least too weak for this situation.

The lose-lose strategy next requires that we have a pity party. I must agree with you that you are inadequate. I am supposed to feel bad for you. Now let's figure out a way that ensures that you won't lose. Why don't we both lose together? Once we all start to believe that we are going to lose we have a great justification for lowering the standards.

Now we dumb-down everyone and declare that we are all winners because we have redefined winning. What was losing before now is winning. You won't have to develop new capabilities. You won't have to step out of your comfort zone. You can be called a winner because what used to be losing now means winning.

In the process we delude ourselves into thinking that no one will feel inadequate anymore because winning is what we needed, not the experience of developing new abilities.

Normally in a competitive environment this doesn't happen. Inadequacy abhors competition. It wants to maintain the status quo. The inadequates of the world would like to see all competition stop. They accept defeat by forfeit, not through competition. They rob themselves of their own power. Thank God we have a world that doesn't operate that way. We have professional sports, business competition, and entertainment where results matter and excuses don't count.

The Karate Kids

During the course of my professional career I have had parents ask me what they can do to enhance their child's self-esteem. Since I didn't specialize in child psychiatry and rarely treated adolescents I referred them for evaluation to others. Often, though, I would try to find out what kind of competition or competitive sports the child was involved in.

It seemed remarkable to me that parents tried to protect their children from competition and shield them from accountability. Why? Didn't they know that the world is a harsh place and their children would have to function as adults? Often I told them the story of a young patient who had deep inadequacies and whose father insisted that he take karate lessons. The young boy had been picked on in school. The more he got picked on the more he developed stomachaches and other somatic symptoms of panic or anxiety. His grades fell, his concentration deteriorated, and his parents started to look to his teachers to protect him from the school bullies.

My recommendation on one occasion was two years of karate with an instructor that the child liked. I emphasized that the child had to attend tournaments with sparring whenever that was possible. It is amazing how quickly a child develops self-esteem when he competes. Even when he is not successful against others, if he is taught to judge his own progress against himself, it soars. The key is discipline. The harder the task the better off the child is.

You need to teach your children that the worst four-letter word is "can't." Teach them that discipline and persistence are good in and of themselves. An old karate instructor once told me that he barks orders so that the children stay alert. "It is important for them to learn to pay keen attention. When they pay attention at the dojo they pay better attention at school."

Some parents are crazy, though. They push their children to compete and then tell them in no uncertain words that they are inadequate when they fail. These crazy parents should be placed in a cage at the Little League competition and an entrance fee should be paid to watch them froth at the mouth when the competition starts. It would pay for new equipment each year.

One of my patients had a father like this. He would decompensate at the sporting events and start screaming. He couldn't keep track of how old his son was. He kept thinking it was himself as an intercollegiate player. The kid switched sports and deliberately chose one his father didn't like.

The worse solution to a child's feelings of inadequacy, though, is to lower standards. We have tried that as a nation. Now we have colleges where high grades are handed out to almost everyone and the college degree means less and less. It has failed as a solution to teaching children who don't learn well. In the process, discipline has gone by the wayside.

With our current obsession with weight and body image we have been developing young people who almost universally believe that they have inherited the wrong body. If you looked at families honestly you would see how the shapes and sizes of bodies are more genetically determined than we are willing to admit. Yet we have this deep need to all have designer bodies. How do some of these people keep such gorgeous figures? Genes. What do we do? We teach our children to feel inadequate over eating habits and the size and shape they are born with. As children become more self-critical in areas where they can't effect a reasonable change they start to feel inadequate and have self-pity. It's the starting point for excuses.

Our kids have role models who make excuses. There are professional athletes who have serious emotional problems and excuse themselves for their violence. The President has so many excuses that the nation ignores them. We make excuses for these people every chance we can. If you are going to bite someone's ear off, apologize and get on with it, but don't tell me you didn't inhale. Children see that and internalize the excuses and then try them out. Or they will take the heroes and superachievers and say, "I can never be that good so I guess I won't even bother to try."

Parents are the greatest source of excuses for the children. The next time you see parents make excuses because they don't want to deal with the emotional consequences of honesty, chew them out for me. Tell them you have my permission.

Every parent would like to have a stress-free life when they raise children. That means every parent is a bit unrealistic. As children see us use inadequacy they learn to incorporate it into their repertoire of justifications for doing what they want, when they want. Making excuses is normal. Allowing the excuse "I am inadequate" is detrimental.

No Shame or Guilt

Part of the problem is that our society has developed this idiotic idea that guilt and shame are bad. Just because they are bad feelings doesn't mean that they are not appropriate and useful. When we do bad things, a good dose of shame and guilt is preventative medicine. To protect children from feeling inadequate some parents decide that they will never shame their children and never make them feel guilty. It sounds like a noble idea. The problem is a person with no shame and no guilt is a sociopath. That's a fancy name for criminal by most people's standards. Holding people accountable is important. Letting them know that they have the ability to meet a higher standard and holding them accountable is the key to overcoming inadequacy. Don't eliminate shame and guilt. Demand performance that creates pride.

What happens to children who have been allowed to claim that they are inadequate and it becomes their lifestyle? They grow up as world-class excuse makers. You probably have some where you work too.

Why Hire When You Can't Fire?

We have become so protective of underachievers in our society that in some workplaces it is almost impossible to fire people. I have been privy to all sorts of stories about poor workplace performance that would make your hair stand on end. That is not the worst part of this character flaw. It is the low productivity by people who feel that they are inadequate but are owed something by everyone else. They have that feeling of entitlement that is often intertwined with excuses.

A middle manager told me a story about his work that happens all across America. He had an employee who was really botching things up. The guy didn't pay attention to instructions. He wasn't interested in anything other than his paycheck. He hated to learn new tasks. It was almost as if he was annoyed that he had to work. The manager was pulling his hair out in frustration because this employee had learned that he could complain about his training. He could claim that it was the company's fault that he was incapable of work. There were so many steps involved to proving that the person should be fired that the manager put up with this nonsense. The union contract had built in provisions for productivity bonuses, and everyone else had to carry the slack. It created huge animosity. Capitalizing on inadequacy is more than just irritating. It can be dangerous and causes work morale

> **Sloth, like rust, consumes faster than labor wears, while the used key is always bright.**
> **—BENJAMIN FRANKLIN**

to plummet. Often, though, people make excuses at work before they even need to. Uncalled for excuses are confessions that a person doesn't want to work.

A patient with deep feelings of inadequacy came to see me after her divorce. The loss of the relationship was devastating, but she was starting to put her life together. Then one of her coworkers came on to her sexually. She made a statement I had heard quite often in my practice. "I didn't have the courage to say no. I couldn't refuse his advances because I felt so inadequate." There are many variations on this theme. "At least someone was showing me attention." Or when it was the boss, "She had the power to fire me so I did what she wanted."

Some superiors in work prey upon people who feel inadequate. They use shame to control them and get them to comply with their wishes. Shame is not necessarily a bad thing unless it is used as a justification for not taking responsibility for one's duty. Bosses who are overly critical love this character flaw. They prey upon people who feel inadequate. They use the excuse makers and their excuses to their own advantage. In the next chapter I'll show you how they do it. For now, suffice it to say that criticizers love the inadequate. What arrogant people fail to realize is that they are just the flip side of the character flaw.

The inadequate excuse maker won't use shame and guilt, failure and ineffectiveness the way you do. Most likely you take a failure as a signal to reassess what you are doing and make some changes. The lose-lose strategy that they have adopted tells them that they are now justified in doing less or nothing.

Behind Every Unsuccessful Man Is a Like-Minded Woman

You have heard the quote that behind every successful man . . . You know the implication; your partner in life is partially responsible for motivating you. I think the original quote was by the British writer,

Thomas R. Dewar, "The road to success is filled with women pushing their husbands along."

The road to failure, though, is filled with partners who use their spouses as an excuse. "My wife suffers from severe inadequacy," the corporate executive with a failed marriage confided in me. He was justifying his relationships with a half a dozen young females. The gentleman preferred women half his age to his wife and children. As the divorce became bloodier he developed some symptoms that caused his internist to refer him to me. Later the internist told me that he had hoped I would be blunt enough to get through to the man. No such luck. His ability to listen was clouded by his lust, a rather common phenomenon for men who feel deeply inadequate when they age. They cope by courting the attention of young "bimbos," as the old internist called them.

"My wife's severe inadequacies have caused me numerous setbacks along the road to success. She can't cope socially and feels really inadequate because she has grown fat while she grew old," the executive told me.

The arrogance he had! She bore children, suffered through the early "hard times," and put up with his self-righteousness. Her payback was receiving his ridicule and criticism. He exercised five days a week and went out with young women. Yet he saw all their problems as hers. Now the hard part to tell you. She helped him set it up.

Rescue Me!

By nature he needed to feel competent and hated to make excuses. He chose as a partner someone who made him feel competent. She was someone whom he could teach how to be as competent as he was. How did he choose her? She needed to be rescued. She liked to stimulate his arrogance, to manipulate him into being the achiever. It made her feel protected.

In the beginning she truly was the woman behind the successful man. It wasn't because she was motivated, though. It was because below the surface she was looking for someone to take care of her needs. That isn't wrong or right. In fact couples take care of each other's needs all the time. What made it a problem was the fact that she had a need to feel loved because she felt inadequate. She started to undermine the relationship through rejection and inadequacy. She wanted someone to prove his love for her by taking up the slack.

Inadequacy makes all sorts of excuses and provides couples the justification for using other character flaws. She suddenly woke up in a bad marriage. People who all of sudden wake up in a relationship that is bad are either in denial or really haven't been asleep to it. It doesn't just suddenly happen.

But suppose you really are addicted to being rescued by others. Self-pity and giving up are your best excuses. You are caught in the unending spiral of shame and guilt, blame and resentment. The characters you wind up associating with really do reflect a like-mindedness. They are other pieces of the same puzzle of character flaws.

The Key to Undiscovered Potential

The beauty of using inadequacy as an excuse for everything lies in the fact that it is the key to undiscovered potential. Locked within the storehouse of abilities that you have been given is a many-faceted diamond. This jewel reflects the talents that the creator has given you for your use in your lifetime. Each of its facets is reflected in some aspect of life where we feel inadequate. The only way we can unlock our potentials is by not making excuses but instead choosing to do what we can with what we have. You must, as the French writer Criel Buysse admonished the peasants in *Sursum Corda*, "Stoop not then to poor excuse."

Yet many of us do stoop to poor excuse, thinking that by doing so we have gained the freedom to be inactive. The key to freedom is activity, not inactivity. In fact the key to unlocking your potential is actively to pursue your dreams. When you are confidently advancing in the pursuit of a worthy ideal you are not necessarily released from your inadequacies. You may actually have to confront them in a more direct way. Your dreams will be delayed, not so much by the obstacles that you encounter but by the excuses you make.

Inadequacy is a great teacher if you are willing to learn. It takes patience and persistence to learn from feelings of inadequacy. It takes tenacious effort even when you are risking failure to be able to move beyond a limiting belief.

> **Have confidence that if you have done a little thing well, you can do a bigger thing well too.**
> **—MALCOLM DAVID STOREY**

Learn something from inadequacy whenever you see it. Learn about yourself and then decide what you have to develop to express the needed capabilities. Often the inability to develop an ability is due to goofy beliefs and not the lack of innate ability. Our deeper issues may be holding us back, forcing us to compare ourselves with some crazy ideal. The ideal may have been planted in your mind by some well-meaning but misguided friend or relative who didn't want to see you hurt. The friend who doesn't believe in you hasn't developed the ability to spot talent. You must learn to do that for yourself. Look for your own talents. Be your own personal talent scout. Sometimes the stress in life is helping you to hone new talents. Sometimes the things we lack are signals that these are the talents we need to learn.

> **There is something that is much more scarce, something finer far, something rarer than ability. It is the ability to recognize ability.**
> **—ELBERT HUBBARD**

Most of our new capabilities develop out of a desire to have or be something more. Giving up the excuse of being inadequate will help you use the talents you have and help you discover the talents that were hidden.

A Declaration of Adequacy!

Many years ago in a woman's group I made patients state "who they were" based on the character flaws that they needed to release. So for instance a young lady named Marilena had for her most prominent character flaw inadequacy. It was her excuse for everything. Without going into long details, she had reason to feel terribly inadequate. Life had repeatedly proven this to her. From her demeaning mother, domineering husband, children who were brighter than she was, to her boss, life gave her feedback that proved that she was inadequate.

Her task in group was to say, "I am adequacy." We tried to allot about half a group session to working with this technique. The rest of the group was supposed to give her feedback as to why she was incongruent or to shout, clap, and cheer in celebration when she said, "I am adequacy" and meant it with every fiber of her being.

> **Consider the postage stamp: its usefulness consists in the ability to stick to one thing till it gets there.**
> **—JOSH BILLINGS**

To be able to release a flaw, you have to face the fact that much of your identity is bound up in the issue of using the defect to manipulate others. It is a way to make life comfortable and secure. It is a way to get people off your back and set you free from responsibility.

A declaration of adequacy from this individual didn't take half a session. It took weeks! After the first two weeks I started to panic because I thought we might have overstepped our bounds. I started praying that she would get it and that the rest of the group would agree. We went a couple more sessions. I kept coming up with a feeling that the group needed it. Finally the breakthrough came. It came with an extra miracle. The other women of the group had processed their issues of adequacy along with her. My patient went on to live a productive life, raise her children, work, and have a loving relationship with her husband. And she never again was willing to accept inadequacy from herself or others.

What we think of ourselves we accept in other people. When we no longer accept inadequacy as an excuse for everything, we stop accepting excuses from other people. We become tenacious in our decisions. When we don't have the capabilities we decide whether it is worth it to develop them. If it is, we go do it. No excuses, just performance and persistence. We push ourselves and discover new limits.

Be persistent in releasing your inadequacy. Almost any excuse can bring it rushing back. When you have broken down an old belief, build new ones. You know the stupidity that we buy into. We've been told that because we belong to a certain race, creed, or clan, we can't do certain things. Build new beliefs based on possibility, not on probability. Ask yourself if it is possible to have or acquire a new ability. You will quickly stop accepting excuses and look for possibilities.

The last thing you want to do is to go to your grave wishing you had done more with your life. Do as much as you can to make your idealized self the one that you have become.

Too Inadequate to Release a Character Flaw

There is a cute excuse that the inadequate use and believe whole-heartedly. It goes like this. "I am too inadequate to be able to release this character flaw of inadequacy." What do you do with someone like that? Take it easy and accept the person at the level that they are at. It's like coaching Little League. You help kids get as far as they are ready. When they learn that lesson and mature, take them a little further.

How does this apply to yourself? Try changing beliefs about inadequacy in some areas, not all areas of your life. Just pick a small belief and change it. Here is how you actually do it.

- Admit you have a limiting belief
- Admit it could possibly be useless
- Put the old belief to rest
- Design a better belief
- Believe the better belief is possible
- Become certain about the new belief

Admit that the belief may not be valid. For some that is a big step. Then store the belief with all the other inadequacies you used to have but don't anymore. For example most of us believed one or more of the following for a while: I can't ride a bike; I'll never learn to use a computer; I may never learn to swim. Design a new belief that would serve you better. For instance if you can't golf but would like to learn, the inadequate belief would be "I am not capable." First start to doubt it: "It might not be true that I am not capable of golfing," then put it to rest. "It is time to realize that 'not capable of golfing' is not true." Next choose a belief that would be more suitable. I am a capable golfer is not a suitable belief, just grandiosity showing you the flip side of inadequacy. You could choose to believe you were capable of learning, or say to yourself, "I believe it is possible for me to learn." Finally you believe that you are definitely capable of learning. "I can certainly learn this game."

> They are able because
> they think they are able.
> —VIRGIL

The pattern is always the same. Inadequate belief—doubt. Then put it out of its misery—retire it. Better belief—it's possible. New belief—I'm certain. Remember Gibbon's famous quote, "The winds and waves are always on the side of the ablest navigators." The capabilities are always coming to those who believe that it is possible.

Virgil knew this truth two thousand years ago. Your spiritual core, or divine identity, true self, whatever you call that part of you that is the still, silent observer within, knows no inadequacy whatsoever.

You are made up of a core of perfect adequacy. Even though everyone has some feelings of inadequacy some of the time, once you realize who you are you will let the feelings go.

Stop making excuses and realize that good old Benjamin Franklin was right when he said, "He that is good for making excuses is seldom good for anything else."

Stop comparing yourself to others and your self-esteem will soar. Stop making your idealized image of yourself in the image and likeness of others. Don't make excuses. Develop capabilities and stop criticizing yourself. You will become far more successful than you ever dreamed. The only thing stopping you is self-criticism, and you don't need to use this next character flaw to haunt yourself.

Stop making excuses and become a person of great capability. More important, become a person of character.

Hypercritical Fault Finders

HOW DO YOU KNOW IF YOU ARE A *HYPERCRITICAL FAULT FINDER?*

1. Are you an expert in finding fault with others?
2. Do you like to keep a list of people's faults and remind them of them whenever you get the opportunity?
3. Do you think cynical is normal?
4. Do you think sarcasm is a social grace?
5. Are you pessimistic about other people's projects?
6. When someone wants to know why something might not work, does that person call you?
7. Did you graduate from law school?
8. Are you better at criticism than solutions?
9. Do you think a massive dose of criticism is a solution?

10. Do you move up the ladder of success by pulling others off?

11. Do you like showing contempt for other's ideas?

12. Is mocking a fun pastime?

13. Do you patronize people who report to you?

14. Do you have trouble in brainstorming sessions because you feel the need to analyze each idea?

15. Do believe life is unfair and it should be pointed out?

16. Do you secretly believe that there are problems but no solutions?

17. Can you zing a person with criticism from across the room?

18. Do you believe it's dangerous to be happy?

19. Do you believe prayer is really an opportunity to complain to God?

In grammar school I had the good fortune of being taught by some rather strict teachers. They were Catholic nuns who learned their teaching methods from an old school that doesn't exist anymore. On a bad day they used the Singapore style of behavioral modification, hard knocks! It worked fairly well. Usually there were only good intentions behind everything they did. They were dedicated and hardworking. They had sacrificed a lot to give the service that they provided.

For eight years there was a problem child in my grammar school classes. He could have been the poster child for ADD but they didn't diagnosis it. Not that he had ADD; he was simply bored most of the time. That's right. The problem child was me. Worse yet there was a bad emotional fit between me and a certain nun who, for the sake of protecting her identity, I will call Sister Justice Tough.

You know the type. Sr. Justice Tough could find something

wrong no matter what I was doing. Everything I did irritated her in some way. She was "just as tough" as she could be with everything and everyone she didn't like. She didn't seem to like Italians at all, which didn't make things easier. At times she really couldn't help herself; it had become a habit to find fault. Whenever I took a test with her it was a challenge to get a good mark because I knew my high grades aggravated her and I earned them.

At graduation I was shocked at the lovely comments she wrote in my book about becoming a doctor. She had related it to Christ and his power to heal. She had already warned me, though, that I would probably be thrown out of high school and not make it to college. That was enough to motivate me to succeed. In fact years later I met her. I was in medical school. I think she found that a bit surprising.

She didn't always exhibit the character flaw of hypercriticism. At times she was right to find fault. She was Justice Tough, gutsy and very strict.

But when she was critical of you she went on a roll. She kept me in detention often, really often. She talked to me about my behavior and character. It was as though she were a steam engine. She would just keep rolling along getting more intense as she got into it. Many of you have had the delightful experience of knowing Sr. Justice Tough. Sometimes she shows up as a boss at work or a frustrated acquaintance trying to deal with life by rejecting you and everything else around her.

I remember a woman who had made some bad choices. She sat in my office and discussed her decision, which was based on her need to be right, intolerance, blame, and desire for vengeance. After she told me what she did, I said to her, "Some people would disagree with that choice."

"What makes you such a hotshot, Doc?" the patient hissed at me. Then she listed a whole series of things that she felt were wrong with me and my character. She went on such a roll that she was emotionally exhausted when she finished. Normally I don't take such things personally. When it is someone close to me it is a little harder to ignore. When it is a client, it is just a symptom, like diarrhea or vomiting. The rule of thumb is to not let it get on you and to clean it up as quickly as possible.

Being cynical, pessimistic, or rejecting is a sign of this character flaw, hypercriticism. Often the surest sign that a person has this flaw is being oversensitive to criticism. This flaw causes people to be so nasty that their criticism is biting or so oversensitive that they feel that they have been bitten by the flaw. The hypercritical person is addicted to finding fault even where there is none. As Henry David Thoreau said, "The fault finder will find faults even in paradise." There is pride in pointing out what's wrong. The hypercritics have an unwritten code that solutions are not necessary, only identification of problems is.

Yet fault finding is an emotionally devastating character flaw. It damages the self-esteem of those who are its recipients. Often it is hidden behind the alleged desire to see someone live their potential, when in fact it is a defense against being judged. Whatever you say about it, it is not something that you have a right to walk around with. I think Julia Moss Seton, in the movie *Holiday,* said it well: "We have no more right to put our discordant states of mind into the lives of those around us and rob them of their sunshine and brightness than we have to enter their houses and steal their silverware."

Good Critics Build

I was told a long time ago that if someone criticizes you, accept what is true and change. Then blow off the rest because it is not your stuff. It has taken me years to learn to respond to criticism that way. Good critics try to build you up. That's why we call it constructive criticism. The great critic is one who learns to criticize himself and not others. Anatole France put it this way, "The good critic is one who adventures among masterpieces." The surest sign that I still need to receive criticism is being sensitive to it.

What we have in this flaw of hypercriticism is a very important mechanism gone haywire. Hardwired into your brain is the ability to see patterns. When something doesn't fit a pattern we get curious. It is a delightful gift from God to marvel and ponder at why things are different. Watch infants. Didn't you always wonder how they could find the piece of lint or the dirt specs on the floor and put them in their mouths? They always find the stuff that doesn't fit or belong. If there is a pattern on the floor and something else is there, they will reach for whatever doesn't fit the pattern. Every little piece of debris that they can find triggers off a mechanism that makes them curious. It is one of the first things that an infant learns to do.

Now take this inborn talent and go forward a bit. Distinguishing patterns then becomes the ability to discriminate what belongs and doesn't, what matches and mismatches. Later we give children toys that cause them to find things that do fit. We teach them how to turn the mechanism around and build. Now if you take a look at what this hardwiring turns into when we become adults you can see just how important it really is. It develops into your ability to judge something as right or wrong, moral or immoral.

Society takes this normal ability and creates troubleshooters, movie critics, and even pure critics like Ralph Nader who look to find fault in industries on behalf of the general public.

Critics do not build. They may show you how you went wrong when you built, but criticism never built a building or painted a painting. Criticism never invents anything, but it may be part of the stimulus or motivation to create. When it operates alone and is an expression of the other character flaws, it is hypercriticism. It is a defect in character that must be addressed. It is related to grandiosity, and rejection of others. When it rears its ugly head as over-sensitivity to criticism being leveled at oneself, it is related to inadequacy and rejection of self. The people you know who are rag-ing indignants, addicted to being right, inadequate—all use hyper-criticism and oversensitivity to navigate the turbulent waters of their relationships.

Demolition Mentality

How often have you had to do a project and then be accountable to some dullard who couldn't get the job done but had managed to get into a position to criticize it? It happens all the time. People like that have the character flaw and then work as hard as they can to get into a position that sets them up to safely use the flaw. They couldn't carry a project to completion if it was finished before they received it. Yet all they can do when they see your work is to criticize your plans. Not having the capacity to see things as they could be, they see things as they shouldn't.

My dad was an avowed dread seeker. He was a funeral director so he had no doubts about how your body wound up at the end of your life. But he was also a cynic who literally fit H. L. Mencken's description, "A cynic is a man who, when he smells flowers, looks around for a coffin." That may have been an occupational hazard, but there are a lot of people out there who are like that and didn't go to embalming school. They have a demolition mentality. They can't build things up; it is against their nature. They have criticized so much and so often that being supportive feels bad to them.

Normally criticism peaks in preadolescence when a child starts to discover that his parents have the ability to make mistakes. The parents come off the pedestal and the child becomes hypercritical. Most parents live through it. We as parents go from being gods in their eyes to being mere mortals. Thank God it is only temporary.

When it doesn't taper off and turn into self-esteem and curiosity about life, you have the makings of a hypercritical individual. It is almost impossible for the person to learn anything. Remember the cynic or the skeptic in school with you? He was so emotionally shut down that his brain couldn't accept new ideas without trying to figure out what was wrong with them.

Demolishing an idea or a dream that someone has before it has been tested is a tragedy. Can you imagine if someone had said to Neil Armstrong, "You can't go to the moon, that's a stupid idea, Neil. Be realistic." Dream stealers are morally and emotionally bankrupt. They are frozen in time just before the present, hoping desperately that their criticisms are right. God forbid that they would have to tolerate new and creative ideas.

Power of the Tongue Is Mightier Than the Teeth

When I outlined the flow of this book I was in a quandary over where to put criticism. It is a character flaw that resembles blame but has a subtle distinction. It actually occurs before blame. By that I mean, psychologically you have to judge and critique before you can blame. Blame seeks to put the focus on the other person's mistake, whereas criticism focuses on its own brilliance. It resembles addicted to being right, but isn't defensive about being right. It is more interested in showing what is wrong. At times it is the prelude to raging indignation but usually doesn't get that worked up. Criticism prefers to disempower you with a word or two rather than try to empower itself like rage and being right do. It comes before or after worry and dread, but often when you have this flaw worry isn't a major issue. In fact there is a sense of security once the cynicism sets it. It may remind you of intolerance, but intolerance rejects you. This flaw rejects your dreams and ambitions. It is as pessimistic as the martyr, but doesn't see itself as necessarily your victim, which is important for the martyr. It is arrogant like self-regard run riot but focuses on your stuff, not on its own.

That having been said, you now have an idea why I waited until nearer the end to introduce this flaw. It holds the key to unlocking the whole pattern of distortion that wreaks havoc on our characters.

Criticism, cynicism, and pessimism link to all the other character flaws and are present in most of us when we use the others. All the flaws are connected and they cascade rapidly from one to the next. They don't necessarily occur in us in the order that I've presented them. Your individual pattern is for you to discover. I will show you how in the last chapter.

Cynics believe people are motivated by selfishness. Being a cynic doesn't give the illusion of power the way some of the other character defects do. It pulls everyone down to the level the cynic is operating on. The fact that it can be done with a sarcastic tone or a different cadence shows how powerful the tongue really is. Long after your teeth fall out the tongue will be around. The tongue is the only sense organ that causes you double trouble. Your senses can contaminate your character by the information or sensations that they take in. The tongue does that too, but it can also wound by the information it gives out. It is truly a two-edged sword. It is more powerful than any weapon of mass destruction.

Achieving Critical Mass!

What are the steps to developing a really negative mental attitude? We know that the ability to be overly critical should taper off and diminish as we get older. But in some people it gets worse as they get older. You know the type. They become bitter and more cynical as they age. They are miserable and cantankerous. They are characterized by the reclusive witchlike lady or the old geezer who hates the children in their neighborhood. They can always find fault with what the children are doing even if it is only playing. They weren't always this way. Let's take a look at the seven steps to developing hypercriticism and becoming chronically cynical.

- I see things as they are
- Life is unfair

- Life owes me a better way, but there is none
- Life is filled with problems and no solutions
- It is dangerous to be happy
- I can't, even if I think I can
- God can't and if He could He wouldn't

I see things as they are. Fault finders claim to be totally realistic. They have the capacity to see things as they are. They tend to err toward the side of pessimism and in the process never quite catch a vision of the world that is marvelous and exciting. Excitement for them is merely sensual stimulation. They are as Ambrose Bierce so aptly stated, ". . . a blackguard whose faulty vision sees things as they are, and not as they ought to be." In actuality a cynic's view leaves out the possibility of change in a world that is constantly changing. Once the critic sees how things "really" are he progresses a bit further.

Life is unfair for these cynics. They have set themselves up with a new rule book that says winning is impossible. The game is stacked against me. I can't possibly live my dreams, even if I had some. This is a miserable way to live. Life is going to knock me down until I am dead. And then God, if He exists, only knows what will happen.

Life owes me a better way, but there is none. Here the pessimistic attitude admits that there might possibly be a better way. Not that he is inclined to create it, just fantasize about its possibility. Critics, though necessary in society, don't create. They measure after the building is done. The only creative critics are those who invent new ways of measuring things, like movie critics choosing the number of stars or thumbs up. Hypercritical types realize that a better way may exist. Rather than find it they sit back assuming that it is owed to them. It may momentarily occur to them that if they want a better way they should figure it out themselves. That's not an option because they suffer from a creativity deficiency. So they make the next-worse choice. They claim that there really isn't a better way, even though they feels it is owed to them.

Life is filled with problems and no solutions. This becomes the mind-set of a life that is drudgery. It is a heavy weight to take on a belief like this. Moving into the future with a pessimistic no-can-do attitude is fatalistic. It further dampens the creative process. When we no longer ask ourselves what could be, what is possible, or how can I make things better, we are stuck with a hopelessly annoying life to put up with. Life feels unfair.

It is dangerous to be happy. Here is how they think: If I am happy I may have to admit that sometimes things get solved; I can gratify my senses and my basic needs, but to be happy about life is dangerous; I will only wind up disappointed.

I have literally had hundreds of patients tell me that it is dangerous to be happy. Most of them were victims of severe trauma. Often they would get annoyed at my positive, upbeat attitude. "Damn it, you're a psychiatrist. You are not supposed to be so happy. You're supposed to be a pessimist like me," a lady once said in session.

"Then I wouldn't believe you'd ever get better. That would make me sad," I told her, "but only for a while. I would start to realize you could be in therapy forever. It would pay for my kids' college education. And I would be right back to being happy again." I could see that her brain ached. So I finished up with, "I'm not that kind of psychiatrist. I believe you can change if you think you can."

I can't even if I think I can. As the pattern sets in and becomes a fixed belief, the mantra becomes I can't even if I think I can. In order to fulfill this belief people set themselves up to fail, even if success would be easier. I have had sales managers tell me that 90 percent of all people who fail at sales don't do the basic minimum required to succeed. Even when they believe they can, they won't so that they keep this rule: I can't even when I think I can.

God can't and if He could He wouldn't. Finally they get to blame the universe. They can't take responsibility for making things better, or worse for that matter. So they blame God, fate, destiny, the universe, their karma, or cosmic law. A young man explained to me that even if God could change things, He wouldn't in his case. I laughed out loud. He thought I was rude. To demonstrate his point he listed all the things he had complained to God about.

> **Complaint is the largest tribute Heaven receives.**
> **—JONATHAN SWIFT**

Complaint to God isn't really prayer. It may be how you pray, but it isn't really part of a healthy pattern. I told the young man that maybe he should try "I can't, God can, I think I'll let him." He thought that was stupid. Letting God be God was an odd concept. The real concept to get, though, is let God be God and be open to becoming an instrument of His will.

Once the skeptic has progressed all the way to the last step in this process the stage is set for chronic misery, flavored with more than a dash of pessimism. The intuition has judged reality as a negative situation. The heart has confirmed the cynicism with pessimistic feelings. The intellect steps in and tries to compensate with criticism.

It feels as right as rain because the whole process of discerning and discriminating is hardwired into your brain. It wasn't hardwired as a character flaw. It was wired in as the ego's method of appraising any reality that didn't match its understanding or preconceptions.

If It Gets Any Worse I'll Scream!

Often being critical is a serious attempt at keeping things from getting any worse. What starts out as an attempt to control becomes a feeling of being out of control in a hostile world. The character flaw has the ability to prove that the world isn't safe. One night during group one of my patients, a young man with relationship trouble, said, "If it gets any worse I'll scream." One of my patients who was an optimist said, "Don't worry, kid, time will make it all work out."

One hypercritical and very sarcastic Staten Islander said, "These idiots don't know how bad it could really get. Let me tell you about it." He went on to give a short discourse on what else could go wrong and what else would go wrong. It was amazing to see. He actually intended to help the young man cope and left him desperate by the time he was finished. I saw the frantic look on his face. He was pleading to the rest of the group for hope. The other group members by that point knew how to diffuse the critic's influence.

Critics impulsively judge a situation and come up with reasons why there is a problem. When it is less than a full-blown character flaw the talent can be used in quality control or law but not in product design or medicine. That is because critics suffer from an emotional and spiritual deficiency.

A Creativity Deficiency

Ralph Nader will never build a great automobile, Siskel and Ebert will never get an Oscar for best director or best actor. They are critics. They have their place in society and are creative in their approach to their areas of expertise. The real creativity is found in the risk taker who sees things as they could be.

The hypercritical suffer from a deficiency of creativity. They are able to see what is wrong and are stuck there. They are not looking to create a better world, but are trying to cope with a rotten one as best they can. They are not the producers or builders in life but those stuck looking over the shoulders of the rest of us who want to try new ideas. It is useless to criticize for the sake of criticizing without producing something better to replace it. The cynic is not interested in replacing anything, just devaluing what you have. That gives you an idea where his self-esteem is. He has to diminish every-thing and everybody in order to feel normal.

It reminds me of a relative of mine who brags constantly. Cri-ticizers will brag when they talk about themselves and then be sarcastic and cynical when they talk about other people's accomplishments. This relative used to brag about being the greatest salesperson. Then later it was the most spiritual person in recovery. Still later it became the most transformed individual in America. The problem was that the person was still tearing everyone else down with that subtle, sarcastic tone. Analyzing everyone else doesn't make you a person who has gone through analysis, nor does going through therapy make you a therapist.

When there is a creativity deficiency the critic criticizes. True creativity doesn't need to knock anyone else to be respected. You don't have to be sarcastic when you speak about a competitor in order to compete. Your behavior will determine the outcome. The critic wants you to form an opinion before you judge the behavior.

My friends Jack Canfield and Mark Victor Hansen of *Chicken Soup for the Soul* fame constantly hear people say that they are going to write a best-seller and surpass them. They are masters at marketing their books. They never criticize anyone else's efforts because they don't have to. They have created hundreds of ways of marketing that no one else ever thought of. Their critics sound hollow and, you guessed it, don't have the creativity that Mark and Jack do.

Whether it is a deep-seated inadequacy or a personality disorder that triggers the character flaw of unhealthy skepticism, undeserved criticism backfires. It may represent false pride or some other issue related to personal identity, but it won't stimulate your creative juices.

A person who is hypercritical and rejecting of other people's ideas is empty and rejecting himself. He is struggling with an emotional void that makes the character flaw seem like it is valuable. No matter how you approach it, unless you are in the demolition business what you build is going to be more valuable than what you tear down.

Pessimistic Attitude

Pessimism is really a global negative attitude toward the present and future. Often its seeds lie in a nasty past, but sometimes it is just a lifestyle that slowly gets more intense the longer you do it. Pessimists see problems as a confirmation that their thinking is accurate. Optimists see problems as hidden opportunity and confirmation that their thinking is correct. They both like to be right.

Suppose being pessimistic was never an option. What would that mean to you? Suppose you didn't allow yourself the luxury of being negative about life? It would certainly be different, wouldn't it?

The pessimist may claim that his or her duty is to keep a wary eye to root out evil. When the character flaw has you, all you can see is evil. It is pervasive and permanent. It is universal. You can't root out everything.

Think about that quote. We find what we suspect, so a critic finds more things wrong as he or she goes unhappily along in a reality filled with problems and no so-

> **We are always paid for our suspicion by finding what we suspect.**
> —HENRY DAVID THOREAU

lutions. Personal relationships are filled with problems. For the optimist they represent a chance for growth and deepening of the relationship. For the critic they are proof that reality is a miserable place to spend the rest of your life.

Pessimistic Partners

You can't be married to a critic. You can't be married to anyone who has any unworkable flaw, especially this one. The harsher the criticism the more it will crack a relationship. To maintain a happy and healthy relationship you must be with someone who is willing to let go of character flaws and work on the virtues. That seems like a tall order for the cynic who believes no one really does that. After all, look at the marriage statistics. Look at all the infidelity and divorce. Opinions that marriage doesn't work anymore are based either on grandiosity or inferiority. People have been making relationships work since the beginning of time. We always will.

"You can't do anything right," a young doctor told his wife in front of my wife, Barbara, and me. "I can't believe I married someone like you."

I was more appalled at the tone than the words. They were biting, but the tone was so harsh, so critical, that my wife and I found ourselves cringing when he said it. We watched as the critic who had a spouse to evaluate slowly worked his way out of a marriage and out of the lives of many of his friends.

"You're such an idiot." I actually heard a wife say in my office. Then she went on a tirade about her husband. She looked at me after she was done with her little performance and with a smile on her face asked me, "Do you see what I mean, Dr. T?"

Her husband interrupted and quietly said, "I must be an idiot." He paused. I think she thought he was agreeing. "I married you, didn't I?"

Marriage with a cynical partner who believes that you aren't capable or that you have stupid ideas and foolish dreams doesn't work. You shouldn't marry a critic unless he or she is criticizing something other than you.

Cynical Parents and Children Without Dreams

What happens to children who grow up in an environment where they are only exposed to criticism and not given solutions to their problems? They become part of the mass of dreamless, visionless humanity struggling to find meaning in a wonderless world. Often the weight of criticism causes them to fear judging things as right or wrong, moral or immoral. They become part of the community of shades of gray thinkers who justify anything if it feels good or is fun. They wouldn't dare confront someone for aberrant behavior because they can't stand to be criticized themselves.

A number of years ago a young lady came to my office. She had tested out at genius level in her aptitude scores. The school psychologist wanted me to prescribe medications for depression. It was the end of her senior year in high school and she had almost flunked out. Her SAT scores were so high that she had been accepted to college in spite of her grades. She was depressed but didn't have quite enough symptoms for me to medicate her. Worse yet her father was a famous colleague at a university center in another state who was going to "evaluate" my treatment. Things didn't improve until she took a job and moved out of the house.

Her father used to tell her, "I am the intelligent one in this house. You will never be as smart as me, nor as streetwise." He even called to explain to me that he was the "great and totally brilliant success story in a very talented family." As Emerson said during a dinner where the keynote speaker must have been a politician, "The louder he talked of his honor, the faster we counted our spoons."

Every dream, every goal, every new idea that had any creative energy was attacked, ridiculed, and destroyed. My patient was never blamed for failing, just assured that she was going to fail. That was supposed to be her lot in life. She couldn't hold a candle to his torch. Just to make sure, he blew her candle out.

"What if your father has been wrong all these years?" I asked her. "What does that mean about your future."

The "father knows best" critic was wrong and his daughter went on to law school. I wouldn't be surprised if she wound up as a specialist in malpractice.

Surgical Air Strikes

During Desert Storm they played a video of a smart bomb guided by laser that went "over the hills and through the glen" right through a small door on a bunker and blew everything up. It was the epitome of a surgical air strike. Afterward every politician in America who knew nothing about military tactics talked about surgical air strikes. It was a dream come

> A cynic can chill and dishearten with a single word.
> —RALPH WALDO EMERSON

true for them. This hypercritical person has the same capability as a smart bomb. That is why he or she likes it.

Peggy from my office used to refer to this ability as removing your appendix from thirty feet with a tongue. You know the type. They are so biting and critical that they can mortally wound you with one word. They are unbelievably dangerous to work with. A word here, a glance there, and they have shredded your hopes, your dreams, or even your good name.

Critics cannot focus on the greatness within you, unless to point out that it is less than they have within themselves. As Henry Ward Beecher said, "The cynic is one who never sees a good quality in a man, and never fails to see a bad one. He is the human owl, vigilant in darkness and blind to light, mousing for vermin, and never seeing noble game."

You should be careful who you place in authority to criticize you. Sometimes it is not possible, but often it is. When you discover that the boss is a cynic you should look to move on. If you are the boss, then you know what you have to do with your employees who are critics. That's right, you fire them as soon as it is reasonably possible. False pride is a common way to compensate for inadequacy by criticizing others. False pride is not what makes a business grow, pride in one's product and performance is. Cynics can't make your business better, only tear it down.

Have you ever noticed how really successful salespeople don't criticize their competition but praise it? They know why their product is better so they don't have to knock down another to make theirs look better. When you have a great restaurant, you don't have to put down others to have clients. Just put out the food and the people will flock to you.

Too Lazy to Solve Problems

You know what happens when people act without dignity. They lower their own character and lose their own values in the process. You lose your dignity when you don't respect the dignity of others. Criticism pushes people away. Most of the time we put down people to look good. This attempt to diminish others has a profound effect on us. It is a negative effect, though. We stop respecting ourselves as we lose respect for others.

I can't help but conclude that sometimes the choice to diminish the dignity of others is made out of laziness. We humiliate others because we are too lazy to look for the good in them and to point out their noble qualities. It takes more energy than we can muster because we don't have the self-esteem. Low self-esteem creates an internal lethargy that disempowers you. It makes you feel like nothing is worth the effort. It is important to resist the desire to criticize. Don't allow yourself to turn cynical and sarcastic.

> It takes a clever man to turn cynic and a wise man to be clever enough not to.
> —FANNIE HURST

A general doesn't become the leader by lowering everyone else's rank but by working on those qualities that elevate his or her character. Criticism is not a leadership skill, unless it is used wisely to gradually erode the negative qualities in others. If not it simply erodes morals and morality.

The Positive Side of Criticism

Yes, there is a positive side to criticism. I would never think to ask you to stop criticizing your children or your friends when they are doing something that needs criticism. I am asking you to consider giving up the sarcasm and the cynicism that goes along with being hypercritical. Criticism requires the ability to make discriminating judgments. Every profession and art requires the skill to criticize. Unless you have the freedom to criticize your spouse or friends, you can't be a complete partner. Your relationship can never rise to the level of a work of art. You can't be a true friend. I lost a dear friend when I realized that he could not hear any of my criticism of his behavior. I made no attempt to judge him. He was doing something wrong. In fact I had made similar mistakes in the past for which I was not proud. I was trying to warn him away from a path that was going to disrupt his life. He chose to let go of the friendship.

You may have to do that, but don't give up your right to be critical as long as you are trying to help someone. The difference is so subtle that often it is lost on the other person. If the person is even a bit oversensitive your critique will seem harsh and unfair.

To help other people with your criticism, make sure you are criticizing behavior, performance, or something measurable. Don't stoop to criticizing feelings and sentiments. It doesn't work unless you have been asked to. How often have you heard someone say, "I can't believe you feel that way." They associate it with, "That was a stupid thing to do." It is much better to point out, "I feel bad that you did that, but I appreciate how you feel about it." I remember early on as a psychiatrist being called on the carpet by my supervisor for judging a patient's emotions rather than trying to understand them. "But they are obviously sick feelings. She is really insane to feel that way," I said.

He kindly looked me in the eye and said, "The patient was dragged in here by the police. Anyone could make that statement you just made, even someone with no training. How are you going to find the meaning for the patient if you sit in judgment? Wouldn't it be appropriate to ask if it is possible that some of her feelings are related to being ill?"

He was right of course. But in some situations you have to criticize and be firm about it. "As far as I can tell that was the wrong thing to do. Let's be honest about the consequences of having that affair." Life will punish your friends and family for the things they do wrong, even if you chose not to. Spare the rod still has some meaning even in a society like ours where we lean too far toward understanding and away from discipline and responsibility.

Criticism is a key to building people. It is the key to correcting mistakes. It is the key to analyzing your efforts and learning from them. One of the astronauts who went to the moon stated that the mission was off course 99 percent of the time. The guidance mechanisms served to evaluate, that is criticize, and then make the corrections. Life should be like that.

Criticism should be rendered with care so you can make recommendations that allow a person to focus on the details that actually need to be changed. Global sarcasm like, "Man, are you off base" is a waste of time. That's the cynic showing his pride rather than the friend getting you on course. It would be better to say, "I think we might be able to find a better way to solve that problem," rather than say, "Boy, that was stupid." I have noticed some of my wiser friends start their messages of wisdom to me with, "Let me tell you about a stupid thing I did and what I had to do to fix the problems I created." Thank God I know so many people who have survived their problems.

If you are on the receiving end, you should embrace all criticism as affection. I am kidding of course, but when you don't take offense to criticism it will empower you. Accepting criticism for something real is useful. It will make a better person out of you. If it is not real, look at the source it came from and then let it be. Getting all upset about it is immature. You are either playing victim or going into raging indignation.

Every valid critique holds the key to a new way of doing things. You have to be open-minded to see it. When you are emotionally mature enough to learn from criticism, then you are really ready to have accelerated emotional growth.

Accept criticism as a friendly gesture, even if others mean to harm you with it. How can they harm you if you benefit from it? Besides, you are probably you own worst critic, aren't you?

Nurturing the Cynic in You!

Let me be the first to admit that everyone has a bit of cynic inside. There is a God-given part of you that has the ability to be cynical, sarcastic, and critical. It will always be there. Is that necessarily bad? What are you going to do about it? How can you transform the work of your inner cynic to be supportive in your personal transformation?

Here is where this all too human trait becomes a valuable asset, an ally as it were in the quest for finer character. It may even be the trait that you use as your signal to stop and do an inventory of your flaws. If the inner cynic worked as your alarm you would be able to make a choice to stop yourself whenever it started. Better yet, criticism may be the character flaw that helps you see when you are going on automatic pilot with one of the other flaws.

The technique is very simple. Stop when you find the mote in someone else's eye.

The Mote in Your Eye Reflects the Beam in Mine

You know the scripture, the mote reflects the beam. What I see in others, I probably have in myself, and need to look at it. I have a friend, Jack, who has been in recovery for decades. He never criticizes young addicts, just helps them. He never tells them what to do, just points out what he did when he was where they are right now.

"I see the good in them and the bad in me," he said to me one night. That's hard to do. It is much easier to do the opposite and see the good in me and the bad in them. "I recognize a lot of things about myself."

WHAT YOU CAN RECOGNIZE WHEN YOU FIND THE MOTE OF CRITICISM IN SOMEONE ELSE:

• Criticism sometimes looks like intolerance

• Criticism can feel like rage

• Sarcasm can sound like addicted to being right

- Complaints, for some, cause contempt, not pity
- Complaints lead to the martyr syndrome
- The cynic has low self-esteem
- Criticism leads to blame
- Sarcasm is just below the surface in self-regard run riot

This character flaw enables you to spot all the others. Once you find yourself getting hypercritical you will find the intolerance, the blame, or the raging indignation. Sarcasm will lead you to understand how you use self-regard run riot. If you can spot cynicism, you can find areas where you are not totally honest about reality. The French say that "skeptics are never deceived." But in fact they are, by their own skepticism.

It's easier if you let the cynic in you respond and be a reminder that you still need to work on yourself.

You Can Do Everything Right!

No one is perfect, I know that. But you can easily go from doing everything wrong to doing everything right. That may appeal to those of you who are ATBR, but I mean doing everything right in a very special way.

Wouldn't you like to do everything right all the time? It is very simple. You need to focus on giving affirmation, approval, or emotional support to others whenever you start to slip into being hypercritical. Practice the spirit of benevolence and emotional generosity. It is possible. I married a woman who does that all the time. She is always telling people that they can succeed, they can be better, that they can do more. It is amazing to watch. I have some friends who do that all the time. Les Brown, Mark Victor Hansen, and Jack Canfield, just to name a few, believe that you have the ability to be more, to live the life you dream of if you are willing to work on yourself.

I have been blessed to run into people who have believed even when I couldn't believe in me. But they all have an underlying secret that they rarely articulate. They are not into the ends justifying the means. They believe in taking charge of your life and doing everything you possibly can but they also believe that you have to be willing to let go and let God. Sometimes you fail, sometimes you succeed, but always, as Charles T. Jones says, "you are learning." You are learning that your character is up to you. If you want to let go of being hypercritical you have to be willing to practice giving approval. Sometimes that means giving approval to others and encouraging their dreams. More often it means giving yourself approval and being accepting of yourself. You spend far more time thinking about yourself than you do about others. You know that is true unless you are a total codependent. You think about your own goals and dreams. Be self-accepting and you will see how quickly that turns into being accepting of others.

Often being accepting may imply allowing yourself to accept the genetic makeup you come with. For some of us it means our bodies. For others it means accepting our intellectual and emotional makeup. But it always means being willing to explore so that you can find out what you are really made of.

See Things as They Ought to Be

In order to reverse the effects of this character flaw you have to be willing to see things as they ought to be, not just as they are. This was a constant conflict for my clients. They were stuck in a reality that had criticized them so much that they were afraid to dream. When life gives you a problem it does so, not for you to be more cynical, but for you to discover your hidden talent. Life tests you so that your true nature can be revealed to you. Do the best you can without being hypercritical and then leave the final results to God.

The Muslims say Inshallah, if God wills it. The idea is that you don't have to beat yourself up if you fall short.

Seeing things as they ought to be will make it easier for you to understand why it is so important to be honest about how things are. Let's move to the last, and perhaps most fundamental flaw of all, dishonesty.

Chronic Dishonesty— The Trap

HOW DO YOU KNOW IF YOU HAVE *CHRONIC DISHONESTY?*

1. Do you lie when it would be simpler to tell the truth?

2. Do you like to see how much you can get away with?

3. Do you believe in the letter of the law rather than the intent?

4. Do you justify your dishonesty?

5. Do you tell people you don't care when you really do?

6. Do you preach morality to others and behave immorally yourself?

7. Do you pretend humility because you think you are better than everyone else?

8. Are the words you speak different from the thoughts you think when you are with people?

9. Do you say one thing but do another?

10. Do you think honest people are naive?

11. Do you believe dishonesty is okay because everyone does it?

12. Do you believe it is okay to lie because you are taking care of your needs?

13. Do you enjoy conning people?

14. Do you think half a truth used to mislead someone is still truth?

15. Do you tell so many stories that you have to have a great memory to keep track of them all?

16. Do you fear you won't be safe if you always tell the truth?

17. Do you lie so much that you have trouble believing other people?

18. Do people need to set up contracts to get you to do what you promised?

19. Has dishonesty adversely affected a relationship with someone you cared for?

I once paid two hundred dollars for a worthless rock. It sits majestically on my bookshelf. My children call it the "Honesty Rock." This large rock was part of a lesson in honesty that I will never forget. I had decided to dedicate the year to truth. One afternoon I was coming back from the New York Institute of NLP (neurolinguistic programming). As usual I was stuck in traffic at the Lincoln Tunnel. We had just purchased one of those 8mm video cameras that were new at the time. The 8mm cassette playback machine was too expensive, so I only bought the camera.

A couple of young men were walking between the lanes of traffic talking to the drivers. They were trying to sell some electronics equipment. I was on the phone with my wife, Barbara, and told her that they had an 8mm cassette player for sale. They wanted only two hundred dollars for the nine-hundred-dollar piece of equipment. She advised me against it. At the last moment I gave the two guys a couple hundred dollars, and then immediately felt guilty that I had just purchased stolen goods. All the way home I was in turmoil. I had never done anything like that before. Secretly I hoped that the thing didn't work and that I could just throw it away.

When I got home I showed Barbara the package, which was tightly shrink-wrapped. I complained to her that I had violated one of my own rules and then reluctantly opened the box. I said to her, "I wish the box were empty and that I was robbed instead," but the box was heavy, just the right weight. When I finally unwrapped it, there was a large piece of granite inside. In grateful relief I carved the letter "H" on the rock and kept it in my office as a reminder that life is easier when you practice honesty. It taught me that old maxim from P. T. Barnum, "Every crowd has a silver lining." I was the silver lining that day. The lesson was worth at least two hundred dollars.

Do You Sometimes Justify Dishonesty? It's a Trap!

The dishonesty trap lulls you into believing that the world would be better, maybe even safer, with a few lies. We all tend to tell them just to guarantee that things work out our way. It causes our souls to become diseased as we fill our lives with complications created by dishonesty. After a while dishonesty becomes a habit.

> **False words are not only evil in themselves, but they infect the soul with evil.**
> **—SOCRATES**

Habitual dishonesty when it would be easier to tell the truth is a sure sign of this character flaw. Chronic lying requires more effort than it is worth. You recognize the chronic liar immediately because you have been burned by lies. No one believes a compulsive liar. In fact no one really likes the charming liar either. We tolerate him just to get what we can. Usually we are promised more than we receive. It takes a while and then most of us learn that it is easier to work with someone who is always honest.

As a character trait dishonesty is expressed as an unwillingness to embrace truth in thought. It effortlessly translates into speech and behavior. It may develop for many reasons, but the bottom line is that the individual doesn't really believe truth is a necessary prerequisite for human interaction. In fact people who chronically avoid the truth feel that they are protecting themselves and others by being dishonest. They suffer a great loss because they can't believe anyone else either.

Spotting the Dishonest Person

You know the old joke, how can you tell when a lawyer is lying? See if his lips are moving. Dishonesty is more often harder to spot. The person possessed by the character flaw, dishonesty, may have some of the following behaviors. Let me caution you, though. These are not universals, and some people are much better at dishonesty than others.

Have you ever heard:

• Someone else is to blame
• This time I'm telling you the truth
• You misunderstood me
• That isn't what I meant when I said . . .
• My intentions were good
• It was an honest attempt to . . .
• Just give me another chance

When people are possessed by this character flaw they always have an excuse. **Someone else is to blame**. I used to get very tired of hearing excuses all the time. One day an Italian-American pasta maker sat in the office, making excuses, right to my face. He was telling about why he hadn't attempted to attend some support groups that I had recommended. He admitted that he needed to go, but his parents wouldn't let him. I told him, "Look, Tony, why don't you just tell me the reason you didn't go was because you had too much ravioli to make." He was quite confused and said, "I don't know what you mean."

I said, "One excuse is as good as another, and ravioli are a lot more interesting than the crap you're trying to feed me right now."

How about, **this time I'm telling you the truth**. Peggy Messina, an experienced counselor in my office, used to cringe when a smooth-talking financial officer from the community would start his sentences with, "I'm going to be honest with you." He was either trying not to lie this time or had lied repeatedly beforehand.

If telling you the truth this time doesn't work, then rest assured that people with this flaw will try and convince you that **it wasn't what they meant** when they said what you heard. Feel confused. You should be. Confusion is one of the little devices a dishonest person uses to stay in control.

Dishonesty takes hold and causes the person to blame everyone else but to claim **his or her intentions were good**. "We didn't know the man was a cocaine dealer," said a presidential spokesperson one day. "When we got here the White House security was terrible." When the person who is a pathological liar is confronted with the truth, he gives you the story that it was an honest attempt to do the right thing. It is trying, unless you have a good sense of humor and don't take it personally. People distort the truth for all sorts of reasons. It may have nothing to do with you. They would lie to someone else if you weren't around. This type would like to stop and can't. They are compulsive just like a gambler or sex addict. And of course **they always want another chance**.

Here are some other clues that can help you spot someone who is using this character flaw.

Do you know people who . . .

- Say they don't care when they should
- Preach morality and behave immorally
- Pretend to be humble but think they are better than everyone else
- Never do exactly what they say they are going to do
- Constantly move their eyes from side to side when recalling what was said
- Think honest people are naive or stupid

We all have had the experience of listening to someone who has been deeply hurt by the behavior of another. It is fairly common to deny it at first. "I don't care what he did. I don't even have feelings anymore," said the mother of four children whose husband had beaten her earlier that day. Actually she was completely shut down and using an emotional safety net called denial. It wasn't true or honest, but it was the best she could do for the moment. Gradually she came to understand how deep her feelings ran. She also was able to face her own anger, resentment, and rage toward a man to whom she had given the best years of her life. Denial is a form of dishonesty that is used to protect us from facing something that is currently too painful to face. In alcoholism denial serves to help the alcoholic continue to drink. That is a necessity for the alcoholic in order for him to stay addicted. It may be his only coping method, and not a good one at all.

Last but not least of all is that idiotic justification that I am sure annoys you as much as it does me: "everybody does it." When my kids offer that to me as an excuse, I make sure that I display a short episode of my temporary "Italian" insanity so that they understand just how stupid it is. Underlying the view that everyone does it is a belief that only the naive tell the truth. If you want to get ahead in life you have to practice deception and deceit. It goes along with a belief that only the dishonest are rich and that the honest have to practice poverty. Yet as Democritus said a couple thousand years ago, "Hope of ill gain is the beginning of loss."

Cross My Heart and Hope to Die

Teaching honesty is one of the fundamental tasks of parenting. It is done by example. It also requires that the child experience punishment for dishonesty, something our society has slowly drifted away from. Some misguided souls even believe punishment was an idea that was useful only for people of the past.

> **Hateful to me as the gates of Hades is that man who hides one thing in his heart and speaks another.**
> **—HOMER**

Dishonesty is the very first flaw that a child learns to consciously use. Little children get delight from playing tricks on their parents. It is a universal experience. Your children will try to see what they can get away with. Hopefully they learn that the consequences of lying are worse than the consequences of the stuff they are trying to cover up. Lying starts early and has to be rooted out early and continuously. I can remember my mom warning us to tell the truth. The punishment for lying to her would be far worse than the punishment for the thing we did wrong.

Mahatma Gandhi's mother used to refrain from eating until she had heard a bird sing at least once during the day. One morning when Gandhi was a small boy he went out to the garden and imitated the call of a bird. He knew his mother was hungry and felt sorry for her. Gandhi's mother caught him faking a birdsong. He was severely punished. She fasted the rest of the day so that he might understand the importance of telling the truth. He never lied again. It was a profoundly valuable lesson that he carried for the rest of his life.

You are a person of fine character when what you do is what you said you would do. More important, you are honest when what you said is what you thought. That is spiritual congruence. Too often we listen to people say something other than what they are thinking and then we watch them do everything but what they promised.

While I was writing this book we were on vacation with the kids. As usual there was more to do than was humanly possible. I didn't take the younger guys to Wet and Wild as my wife and I had promised. One of my children said, "You promised. You should be more careful about what you promise, because you could disappoint a child."

I have to admit he was right. We went the next day.

Most dishonesty starts with a belief that a basic need is not going to be taken care of. A successful female executive from a large corporation had a chronic need for recognition. She had to struggle to keep from exaggerating at work. She desperately wanted her coworkers to appreciate her. There is nothing wrong with taking care of our own needs, but when we exaggerate, we slowly develop the belief that it is okay to be dishonest in order to take care of ourselves. Some of us exaggerate, embellish, or stretch the truth just to add a little drama to life. That's what causes a lot of our problems.

Honesty is one of those virtues or wholesome qualities that can be practiced just about anywhere. It makes the world a better place. Truth is the foundation of society. It makes your life easier. From ancient times we have known this.

From the Boy Who Cried Wolf to Liar-Liar

One of the first fairy tales that little children hear is the story of the boy who cried wolf. You know the fable. The little boy is bored watching his sheep so he comes up with the idea of playing a game of lying to the townspeople about a wolf attacking his flock. He runs to town, sounds the alarm. They all run back to the meadow and, lo and behold, no wolf. He does this a few more times, thoroughly enjoying his own antics. Finally when the wolf does appear, no one will run to his aid. Children need to be told this story. More important they hear the story at that precise time in their life when they discover that people can lie. But even adults need to be reminded of the importance of truth. Entire cultures have been established on foundations of truth. The Judeo-Christian ethic based on the Ten Commandments admonishes, "Thou shalt not bear false witness." Modern man has redefined this as "don't get caught telling a lie." We have let this degenerate to where it is necessary to put every detail into a business contract. If there is a way of stretching the truth, people will. If modern man has given his word to do something, he generally doesn't do it unless it is in the contract. How different from a century ago, when a settler in the western United States would shake on it and give you his word.

Dishonesty is committed in steps. First of all a person has to have a belief that unless he lies his needs won't be taken care of. The need has to be important enough to lie for. How often do you see teenagers lie to each other about what they have done, just so that they might fit in.

Pinocchio is another great fairy tale that tells the story of a young boy who has to struggle with the consequences of lying and the rewards of telling the truth. Isn't it interesting that he can only become Geppetto's real live son when he is truthful?

The other night I was watching the evening news. I have this annoying habit of listening to politicians speak as though I am listening to patients, especially drug-addicted patients. Often the politician is deliberately dishonest, by telling half a truth. Worse yet the "leaders" enjoy their own con. Watch a politician or front man for someone get asked a question and smile, because he has prepared a lie for it already. Some of our more famous Americans are especially good at it. The media needs politicians for stories. When the chronically dishonest person is in a relationship with someone who badly needs that relationship, as the media does with politicians, it is a formula for disaster.

Lying is not limited to drug addicts and politicians, but certainly is more obvious with these two groups. Dishonesty is a way of life for many people. It taxes their emotional resources and puts a great strain on their memory. Not to mention that most of us find dishonesty tests our patience.

Hinduism has a great epic tale called the *Rāmāyana*. In it Lord Rama goes into the jungle for a period of fourteen years so that his father's word will not be broken. The *Rāmāyana* is an epic tale of God incarnated as a prince who gives up his right to the throne in order to help his father keep his word. The story is a great reminder that it is a spiritual duty to tell the truth. How many of you believe that our modern-day princes in Washington, D.C., would be that scrupulous? We now believe that all politicians lie. Honesty used to be a criterion for selecting a person to represent you in public office. We all have heard Lincoln referred to as Honest Abe. Wasn't it Lincoln who said, "You may fool all the people some of the time; you can even fool some of the people all of the time; but you can't fool all of the people all the time"?

Everyone knows the story of George Washington and the cherry tree. The founder of our country could not tell a lie. That story may be myth, but it represents the need for our society to be based on truth. Truth in word and deed is the foundation for society. Truth is the foundation for your relationships. If you are currently in or have ever been in a relationship that has many secrets you know what I am talking about. Living a lie is really difficult, though people with this character defect are good at lying to themselves about how dishonest they are.

Dishonesty occurs on many levels. It starts on the level of thought and is particularly difficult to recognize because we can easily deny that we are being dishonest. Dishonesty seems to be most obviously associated with language. As soon as you learned to speak, you probably tried to "lie." It is normal to test truth. That is far different than an adult lying when he could just as easily have told the truth. That's a behavior that shows that you are stuck in a childish pattern.

Behavior is where dishonesty as a flaw can be most easily confronted. It shows up as stealing, cheating, adultery, and simply ignoring the things we ought do when we should do them. It translates to broken promises, saying one thing, meaning another, and doing a third. Dishonest behavior may be selfish, or greed or fear based, but invariably it comes with some sort of self-serving justification.

The Tangled Web We Weave

I never met a drug addict who started out to become addicted. They all just wanted to have a little fun or fit in with the crowd. None of them started to use drugs so that they could get AIDS or infect their families with the virus. There was that little white lie they all told themselves: a little won't hurt me. I can quit tomorrow.

> **The liar's punishment is not in the least that he is not believed, but that he cannot believe anyone else.**
> **—GEORGE BERNARD SHAW**

White lies seem so innocuous. It is where they lead that is the problem. Sometimes we tell lies to protect our children and then later suffer the consequences. A gentleman came to my office to talk about explaining to his children who their mother was and why she had left. He had been telling them lies for years to protect them. She had left to go back to Las Vegas and work as a dancer. He told them that she had died. His family members lied with him. The patient feared that if they knew the truth his children would develop their "wild streak" and become like their mother. He had developed such a tangled web that he said to me, "Doc, if I start telling the truth now it will only complicate things more."

He believed it too! But he could not keep them from finding out the truth from other relatives.

When we deliberately decide to be dishonest it often snowballs into a lot more than we expect. It is a seemingly unending process.

Truth is the basis of society. There is no trust without truth.

There are no relationships without trust. There is no family without relationships, and no community without family.

Telling the truth actually is a lot simpler for most people. It requires less emotional energy and certainly a less-developed memory.

"I didn't know telling the truth would be so difficult," a young boxer with an addiction that ruined his career said to me. He thought that telling the truth was for the naive. He was a tough guy. The more he lied the harder life became. He finally had to face his fear of truth. Only in the ring could he be honest with his fists.

Distorted Beliefs/Distorted Truths

Did you know that there is always a good intention behind a lie? The road to hell is paved with them. Just because people claim that they meant well shouldn't get them off the hook for distorting the truth. Actually, you can help those who have distorted the truth to serve their purpose by holding them accountable and allowing reality to beat them up a bit. It is the most compassionate thing that you can do.

Every flaw that you or someone you know uses is an attempt to take care of a need. Most compulsively dishonest people are scared to death and can't cope well. Just think, they constantly have to try to figure out what lie or distortion is going to protect them or one of their needs. What a way to live. On top of all of this is the need to have a great memory so they can remember what they said to whom. It really is a high-maintenance way of living.

> One ought to have a good memory when he has told a lie.
> —PIERRE CORNEILLE

That is why many of the great deceivers, the spinmeisters, the corrupt and deceptive, are so intelligent. They have to be, in order to remember their version of reality. Their view of the world is a reflection of their own inner poverty. They have to steal to be rich, manipulate to be in a relationship, embellish to be appreciated, and distort so that you only see their point of view.

Yet there is always that good intention, that desire to create wholeness that is pushing them to dishonesty. I don't condone it at all. I just understand it.

Untangling the Web

The tangled web is spun by those who believe dishonesty is useful. It is part of a defense and may be the only way the person with this flaw can cope for now.

It is very important how you respond to it. You need to respond and not react to dishonesty. All character flaws have a subtle goal of control. When you react to someone else's flaw you are giving it control.

HOW TO DEAL WITH THE DISHONESTY FLAW IN OTHERS

- Set up contracts with the honesty impaired
- Be specific when making agreements
- When you notice the lie remember it may be the best that they can do
- Remember that often they can no longer recognize that they are lying
- Understand how it relates to one of the four needs
- Don't get angry, get tough
- Don't ever cover up others' lies
- Let them wallow in their chaos
- Be compassionate—hold them strictly accountable
- Sever relationships and be firm

I understand everyone occasionally uses dishonesty or is tempted to, but here we are talking about the person who is possessed by the flaw, not one who possesses it. We are seeking useful strategies for dealing with the honesty impaired. Your best bet is to set a good example and not try to manipulate in your relationships.

The best thing is to show dishonest people that you can be trusted. This eventually comes down to showing them that you can be trusted to hold them accountable.

Set up contracts with the honesty impaired. We develop written contracts with patients so that we remind them of what they promised to change, or promised to do. I am sorry to inform you that often you will have to have contracts with the honesty impaired. **Be specific when making agreements**. This character flaw uses language the way a magician uses a wand. "I will lower taxes for the middle class," say politicians out of one side of their mouths. "And furthermore, if elected we will give a whole new meaning to 'middle class,'" they say out the other.

The only guarantee you have is that eventually the honesty impaired will lie to you. **When you notice the lie remember it may be the best that they can do**. It was probably the best that they were capable of at the moment. Don't be offended, don't react. Respond. **Remember that often they can no longer recognize that they are lying**. Sometimes their denial is so great that it doesn't compute as dishonesty, just their point of view. I can remember doing home interventions with families of alcoholics. Father Angelo, a priest who worked with Mother Teresa, accompanied me on some of them as part of his training in addictions. He was marveling at how badly one of the interventions went and said, "This person really can't see the problems his drinking is causing. It is impossible for his mind to conceive it."

Understand how it relates to one of the four needs. It is important to see that the dishonesty relates to one of the four basic needs: approval, belonging/love, freedom, and fun. If you can figure it out, good. It will help you understand how to help the chronically dishonest suffer consequences.

Get tough. Love can be tough on people when the issue is integrity. Friends have the right to be brutally honest if it will save others from the consequences of ill-thought plans or immoral behavior. Get very tough and **don't cover up for them either**. It would be dishonest to participate with them. How often are you let in on secrets by your friends that require covering up? If you care for the person who has been dishonest it is better to **let them wallow in the chaos** that they are creating. Don't get involved and don't get angry. Get tough.

Hold them accountable. It really is better for someone to learn accountability. The younger they learn it the better it is. If they can't accept it, move on. **Sever relationships and be firm**. It is okay to sever relationships with people whose flaws keep it from being a working relationship. You are showing the person that you can be trusted to leave if there is no relationship.

When you work on being honest you are teaching by example.

Work on Yourself

IF YOU OR SOMEONE YOU KNOW HAS HAD A PROBLEM WITH DISHONESTY HERE IS WHAT YOU NEED TO DO:

- Work on being honest one day at a time—be gentle
- Practice honesty in all the little things you say and do
- If and when you do lie, quickly admit it, even if you only exaggerated
- Make amends to people you have lied to directly
- Commit to truth in the future with these people
- Trust that you will be safe if you are honest
- Identify the need you tried to fulfill by being dishonest

- Identify the goofy belief that justified lying
- Find a new belief that could take care of your need, e.g., to belong
- Use honesty to support the belief

Start today **working on being honest one day at a time**. Remember that if this flaw is deeply rooted then you must be gentle with yourself. The still, silent voice within whispers to us when we are dishonest. I know that you have heard it. It will remind you when you have been dishonest even in **the little things you say and do**.

But what do you do if you slip and tell a lie, behave in a dishonest way, or mislead someone? **If you do lie, go ahead and admit it**. I had a patient who was a carpenter. He misled everyone for no real reason other than that it was a compulsion to lie. He had lied so often that telling the truth never felt right. He finally vowed that whenever he lied to someone, he was going to tell them that he had lied. He hated to admit it, but he did it quickly, every time. Some of his friends started demanding that he fess up whenever they suspected he had lied. They all knew when. They had always seen through his stories. In a few days his behavior dramatically changed. He got sick and tired of admitting it all day long.

To those you have lied to, make direct amends. Let me give you my personal definition of amends. A direct amend is when you practice the exact opposite of the character flaw you used. For someone addicted to being right a direct amend would be admitting you are wrong. For someone who chronically assigns blame, it is accepting responsibility. So for dishonesty the best amends is to repair old damage and to commit to practicing honesty and truth with those you have offended. **Commit to truth in the future** with those you have lied to.

The hard part for some is changing the belief that lying protects us. **Trusting that you will be safe if you are honest** takes courage. It may be scary at first, but with a little practice you can do it. For those of you who have had to lie to avoid abuse, it is understandable that trust comes at a great price. It has been my experience that developing trust has a great payoff. You will have new relationships that are based on honesty.

Look to the need you are trying to fulfill through being dishonest. Was it belonging, appreciation, freedom, or fun? There is usually **a goofy belief that justified your being dishonest**, so that your need would be fulfilled. Find a new belief and be honest about it. If you can **support your new belief with honesty** the pattern of deception will fade away quickly. Be gentle with yourself. You don't have to be strong to change, just willing.

Honest, and You Can Take That to the Bank!

Let me digress for a moment. I would be naive to say that honesty is the best policy because it is easier. In fact it is often harder. It just makes the overall working of our relationships, and ultimately society, easier. We learn at a young age that sometimes honesty is very difficult. That is part of why it is esteemed in a person's character.

Without great character your gifts and talents are susceptible to misuse. They become tools for your character flaws to abuse. Great wealth is only useful to you if you are of great character. If you accumulate riches without character you will be imprisoned by them because they empower your flaws.

Dishonesty is a trap that uses the desire to be wealthy to hook you. Not that I have anything against wealth. It is your right to create it. It is just that if you create it through your flaws it will destroy your character. Most of the very wealthy people I know are about as happy now as they were when they were broke. Some are very happy too!

Truth and Consequences

My patients frequently complained that it isn't easy to be truthful all the time. In fact when we testify under oath we say, "so help me God," because it has been assumed forever that God is the only one that could help you to be totally truthful. I am often amazed at the freedom a person feels when he or she gives up the right to lie. "Sathya," or "truth," in Sanskrit is one of the 1,008 names of God. I believe that truth is a gift or grace from God.

The truth is that practicing honesty is the key to breaking the control the other character flaws have over you. The consequence of even a little willingness to change is a profound, long-lasting trans-formation. It may seem subtle at first, but over a period of time the habit of truth replaces the compulsion of dishonesty. Life becomes easier, simpler, more peaceful.

Dishonesty is really the fundamental issue behind each of the other character flaws. It is the foundational flaw upon which we can create the need to use other flaws. I saved it for last because it is often very difficult to face. Once you break through with honesty, releasing the other flaws becomes easier.

Dishonesty is never the sole problem in a person's life. In fact most of the time it is part of the hidden pattern of how you create your problems. Even though dishonesty is not the sole problem it is part of each character flaw. Truth is a universal part of the solution.

Dishonesty masked as denial allows us to maintain the other flaws. Make truth the foundation for looking at all the other char-acter defects. The ideas in this book will become simple; not easy, but at least simple.

Let me quickly address the idea of "faking it till you make it." This is not really dishonesty but an adaptive process to try and work out strategies to succeed. We all pretend that we are who we are going to be. I was a doctor in my mind a long time before I ever went to medical school. You don't have to give up future goals to be honest, but you do have to be honest about paying the price to reach them.

Dishonesty doesn't leave you because you push it aside. It isn't the struggle that causes you to win this battle. It is embracing the truth and holding on until you finally understand that all your needs will be better taken care of by truth than by dishonesty.

Dishonesty with God is an issue you need to look at before turning to the next chapter. My patients who had a real belief in a higher power to whom they were accountable seemed to get the honesty idea quicker. If you have issues with God as you currently understand Him I'll offer some simple suggestions to you. Surrender in every religion brings profound peace. Simply stated, dishonesty is the primary flaw that impedes the capacity to surrender.

Dishonesty is almost impossible to get rid of without willingness to change, but it must be accompanied by some open-mindedness too. You need to be open-minded in order to see the possibilities that exist around you.

Seeing things as they ought to be will make it easier for you to understand what it is you are here for. You have some sort of destiny, some purpose that you were born to. You can only find it and create it through your character. As Heraclitis said, "A man's character is his destiny." You can change your destiny only by changing your character. And that idea brings us to the last chapter.

Change Your Character, Change Your Destiny!

HOW CAN YOU TELL PEOPLE WITH FLAWLESS CHARACTERS?

1. Do they exhibit heroic virtues?
2. Do they love and accept others in spite of all those flaws?
3. Do they gently demand that you change for the better?
4. Do they seek accountability over rights?
5. Do they keep their word?
6. Are they kind enough to be judgmental only of your behavior and accepting of your being?
7. Do they find solutions rather than problems?
8. Do they fix the problem rather than the blame?
9. Does it take a lot for them to get upset?

10. Do they let go of grudges and resentments?

11. Are they generous, offering a hand up not a handout?

12. Are they scrupulously honest?

13. Do they assume that you are adequate?

14. Are they peaceful, tolerant, and hopeful?

15. Do they refuse to act like victims?

16. Are they dreamers, encouraging others to build a better world?

17. Do they speak to and touch your flawless self?

18. When they are wrong, do they quickly admit it?

19. Are love and duty the foundations of their actions?

"Who are you really?" I asked this question of one of my patients in group. I was in a kind of reverie, an altered state of consciousness. I wasn't sure why it happened, but I went along with it hoping it would help me get to the bottom of why this patient hadn't made much progress. It was as though time had suddenly stood still, and we were in a spaceship hurtling through space. Nothing else existed but the people in this group and a power greater than myself to whom I had surrendered and found myself at peace.

"What is your spiritual core made of?" I asked the bewildered young lady. "Your know the age-old question. Who are you at the depth of your being?" I couldn't answer for her. All I could do was point out that she wasn't the words she spoke, the things she did, the feelings or thoughts either. I could sense it clearly because I had melted into a timeless zone of pure love. The past and future had vanished. I was being, awareness, and bliss, playing the role of Dr. T. I sat and observed, expecting a miracle.

"You are the witness of all this, the silent observer who has seen years of insane behavior with drugs, sex, and money. You are the being who noticed what was going on, without judging, eternally at peace, untouched by the deep sorrows that you have known," I said. I watched the room sparkle as though my vision had suddenly become clearer. The patient had made little progress and was struggling to allow herself to be that spiritual being who could work on her character and not fail. She was discouraged, until that night.

All of a sudden she started to talk, to ramble on about years of abuse by the men of her family, those entrusted to raise her. In a long, slow moment the deep secrets that had kept her sick came pouring out. There was so much pain that I hadn't known about. She had chosen to hide it all from me and her primary therapist. She was afraid of our judgment of her. So much pain and suffering and yet it was relinquished in a moment of pure forgiveness. That night it no longer mattered. She had discovered that her true identity, her spiritual core, had been "flawless" the whole time. She had realized who, or "what" she really was. A power awoke that evening in someone who had never known spiritual power. She was free, liberated by the knowledge of who she was. She had touched upon her "flawless self." She didn't have to forgive and forget. She had tried that for years. The moment she realized her flawless self she became forgiveness. She knew her spiritual core was blameless, just the witness. Her ego had used her character flaws. That night from within the experience of forgiveness and blamelessness her task was completed.

Your true nature is flawless too. You are a being of immeasurable virtue, filled with wholesome qualities waiting to be tapped and used for the benefit of humankind. You are a being of bliss and awareness. You might not have realized it yet, but you are. You may feel sad and confused today, but trust me, your core, your true identity is absolute joy and awareness.

You may not realize this truth, but trust me it is true. Trust, by the way, is a choice. I know it may sound a little strange, but trust is a choice you make in so many things. If I am right, you have the potential to release all your character flaws and experience a joyful and peaceful life. Something deep inside you, your flawless self, already knows that I am right and that you can have it if you are willing. The flawless self of everyone else is made of the same stuff as you are. Their egos may use character flaws, but the core of their being is blameless. Knowing this leaves you with an option. That is joy and peace.

> Try not to become a man
> of success but rather try
> to become a man of value.
> —ALBERT EINSTEIN

That should be your goal, joy and peace. You should strive to be a person of great character because no matter what happens to you, you will experience a life of peacefulness. Notice I didn't say a life without problems or situations involving your body and mind, but a peacefulness in spite of appearances.

How Do You Know You Are Making Progress?

Sometimes it is difficult to realize that the transformation has started to take place. When I first entered a recovery program I had to face my character defects. I had to become willing to change. Deep character change requires patience and humility. For most of us, those qualities take years to learn. We think because we feel impatient that we are not learning anything. Don't be misled by your feelings. Transformation is as inevitable as the bloom on a rose.

One night I got called to the emergency room to see a patient on whom I had done only one consult a few years before. He was asking for help, something that he had refused repeatedly. And not just from me either. He had refused to seek any kind of help from all the other psychiatrists who were on staff.

"I am ready, Dr. T," he said. "The last time through the ER something you said ruined my ability to continue my insanity."

I couldn't remember what I had said. It probably wasn't important for me to remember, just important for the patient. He was an alcoholic who had continued to drink but was now ready to stop. When a person is ready the lessons come from everywhere. It doesn't matter who or where. When you are ready to give up a character flaw it is like the alcoholic who has gone to one too many AA meetings. Drinking no longer is fun. With character flaws, they are no longer fun when you are ready to release them. We get frustrated and can't quite get back to enjoying them. Here is a secret, though. When you are entirely ready to release them they get removed. That's right. At first they lose their attraction. Later they get pulled by the grace of God. I don't have any better explanation for it. Even if I could invent a psychological explanation for it, I wouldn't bother. I have seen it happen too often to know that explaining willingness doesn't really make willingness happen.

What I am willing to do, though, is to give you the pattern, or the reality response, as I call it in my seminars. Once you learn it, you can use it for any character flaw you wish. I have been describing it throughout this book so it will be easy to understand. It is part of what I see as the seven phases of character development.

> **Our strength grows out of our weakness.**
> **—RALPH WALDO EMERSON**

It is precisely in our areas of greatest weakness that our strength of character develops. All through this book I have been trying to show you how that happens. At first the phenomenon is an annoyance to you because you start to notice that you're not perfect. In fact it is irritating to the ego to have to admit imperfection. The imperfection is not who you are. When we get good at recognizing character flaws, then we start being an irritation to everyone else around us. You know what happens, the convert becomes the fanatic. The person who finds out about incest starts the healing process and then becomes obsessed with telling everyone about it. The alcoholic who is new in program starts to tell everyone else about his or her drinking. The patterns we find in ourselves start to become very noticeable in everyone else that has them. At this juncture you risk losing friends by pointing out their flaws. That is why you need to move on to developing patience and some prudence in dealing with them.

The mark of perfection is the tolerance of the imperfections of others. When you first start working on character transformation you don't see that your self is flawless already. Your ego has the flaws and uses them for survival. Your intolerance of the flaws in yourself and others is just a starting point. If you still get irritable with yourself and others over the flaws, you have some work to do.

We notice our weakness and then respond by developing the strength to balance it out. In our greatest flaw comes the realization of who we are, if we are willing to change. True emotional and spiritual strength comes from the admission of weakness. Spiritual strength requires surrender. In the context of flawlessness it means the ego surrendering its right to use character flaws. Then it must develop the willingness to use the tools that one's flawless self has had all along, our virtues. As Sathya Sai Baba, the Indian avatar said in a discourse to young students, this is what God wants from us, ". . . the flowers blossoming on the tree of man's own life, fed and fostered by his own skill and sincerity. They are the flowers of his virtues grown in the garden of his heart."

It is your duty to transform yourself in the areas of your greatest weakness. It can be done by a balance of surrender and grace. It is expressed through what I have referred to as spiritual congruence, being aligned in thought, word, and deed. This is what is known as moral behavior. Oddly, we live in a time when so much progress has been made in information processing but not morality. Every idea in the universe is flying around on the Internet. Morals and morality have been relegated to a secondary position in man's life. Your character and your morals are supposedly your business. It is assumed that before you go for a drive around the information superhighway in cyberspace the little issues of morality are already taught, learned, and practiced. We focus not on morality but the fulfillment of desires.

Morality is the behavior that reflects your character. Your morality is witnessed by others by the deeds you do for others. Morality is fundamentally about a reverence for life. The great Albert Schweitzer said, "Ethics, too, are nothing but reverence for life. That is what gives me the fundamental principle of morality, namely, that good consists in maintaining, promoting, and enhancing life, and that destroying, injuring, and limiting life are evil." The most limiting thing we do in our culture is to cater to the flaws of one's character rather than demand high character. We are still at a primitive level of functioning if we don't make spiritual congruence and integrity a top priority. Society won't demand it of you, therefore you must demand it of yourself.

How Can You Spot a Person with Good Character?

This has been a difficult question for me. Often we are misled by trends, current fads, and media attention on what turns out to be the superficial aspects of a person's character. Good character is hard to determine. You have to see how a person handles the seasons of life. In the end judging someone else is really a waste of time. Our society uses fame and fortune as a measure. That too is useless. Michel de Montaigne reminds us that "even on the most exalted throne in the world we are only sitting on our own bottom."

> All sects are different, because they come from men; morality is everywhere the same, because it comes from God.
> **—VOLTAIRE**

Character is the clothing that your flawless self wears. It is the vestment that your soul puts on in order to carry out the duties of this experience we call life. There are, however, seven signs or marks of character. I will touch on them so that it will be easier for you to judge your own character development. The marks of character are also useful in helping you spot a person of good character. Not to judge them with, but to decide whom you should associate with. Character transformation often occurs in groups of people working together toward a harmonious goal. I don't believe that you must stay only within your social or religious environment to find people of good character. They are everywhere in every society and every religion.

The greatest mark of character is surrender. Even Christ uttered the words, "Not my will but thine." Surrender to divine will is the mark of greatness of character. It is the mechanism that opens the door to this marvelous experience of grace. It is the prayer: "Speak but the word and my soul shall be healed." Since all our flaws are intertwined it takes a shower of grace to see us through them. But like the rain, grace falls on all of us. If you plant the seeds, the flowers of virtue will blossom.

Your flawless self will express the wholesome qualities that make up your character. Just as the flaws cluster together, so do your virtues. Intolerance and vengeance show their ugly heads one after the other, but so do tolerance and forgiveness. All the virtues harmoniously work if you work on releasing even just one of the flaws.

Those Holes in Your Soul!

What about those holes? What happens to them when you start this journey of transformation? They become conduits like the heads on a sprinkler system. Love, peace, forgiveness, whatever it was you lacked, flows through the holes in your soul and sprinkles the people in your world. You become a channel of these divine qualities. Your character gives off these qualities because they are who you are. Let's take a look at one of the divine qualities that you are made of.

You Are Happiness—Beware of Those Bliss Busters

If you are like most of us, you have been running around trying to get happy through various means. When you unveil your flawless self you are happiness. There is nothing to get. You realize that the being within who was witnessing all the turmoil in your life was never happy but was actually the happiness itself. You wanted happiness but went about it with the following bliss-busting attitudes.

- I want to be happy (I am not)
- I do not want anyone between me and my happiness
- Only I must be happy (if only I can possess it)
- I am happy with . . . (I don't have it, though)
- I can be happy (I am not now capable)
- I want someone else's happiness (mine isn't good enough)

It takes a part of you, that part that notices when you feel happy and when you feel sad, for you to understand what the six bliss busters are about. Each of them requires you to pursue happiness as though it were a state to be achieved by having something that you lack. That is because most of us agree with Robert Green Ingersoll when he says, "Happiness is not a reward—it is a consequence. Suffering is not a punishment—it is a result." We think that cheerfulness is really what bliss is all about. "Cheerfulness, in most cheerful people, is the rich and satisfying result of strenuous discipline," points out Edwin Percy Whipple. But bliss is none of this. It is closer to the view of the father of the atom bomb, J. Robert Oppenheimer. "The foolish man seeks happiness in the distance, the wise grows it under his feet." Let me paraphrase it and say that being happy is what you get when you let who you are determine your choices. Who you are is bliss, perfect happiness, and peace. Why look for it somewhere else when it is within you the whole time? How do you find it? You take the mask off. Take off the armor that you wear to protect yourself from others. Remove your character flaws. The part of you that notices when you feel happy and when you feel sad knows the truth.

THE SEVEN PHASES OF CHARACTER DEVELOPMENT

- Trust who you are
- Accept responsibility

- Ask the questions of character
- Work with reality
- Develop great beliefs that reflect great character
- Use virtues
- Associate with those who show signs of character

Trust who you are. It is an important choice. Most people fear trusting that they are the eternal inner witness who silently observes reality. That is because they fear for their lives! That's right. We are all trying to survive this thing called life as best we can. Being raised above a funeral parlor taught me that we aren't going to make it through life with our bodies alive. Nobody does. But so what? That's the small stuff. There is so much more to you than your body and your constantly busy mind. It is time you started being who you are.

Accept responsibility. If you are like me you are a bit out of step with modern society. All people are trying to protect their rights, dividing themselves into little groups of people with special needs and special privileges. Here is a new group for you to join—those who gratefully accept responsibility for their actions and live a life of duty.

Okay, that doesn't sound like much fun to me either, but when you run into a moral dilemma, and you will, this is the group to belong to. They are the ones who never lose their joy. There can be no privileges without responsibility anyhow, so you may as well accept that. It is the second phase of character transformation. The next time you have a moral dilemma, such as conflicting loyalties, see how much easier it is when you take the high ground and accept responsibility.

Ask the questions of character. If you don't ask the right questions you wind up getting the wrong answers. That is why all the nightly news surveys are so silly. They decide what they would like to find out and then ask the questions. You do the same thing but most of the time it is unconscious. We ask ourselves silly questions that don't polish our character.

For instance our society emphasizes the question, Am I going to enjoy this? A flawless character asks, Is this acceptable behavior for me? The character flaw dishonestly looks at a situation and asks, Can I really get away with this? The flawless self asks, Does this conform to my values?

Here are a few more questions you should ask along the way.

- Am I being honest about this?
- Is this choice going to hurt anyone?
- Is it going to help others?
- Am I practicing love and nonviolence with this choice?
- Am I peaceful with this choice?
- Am I doing this for my ego or for the benefit of others?
- Am I spiritually congruent?

Perhaps the most frequent question that you have been asking yourself is, Can I get this stuff Dr. T is writing about or am I going to stay confused forever?

The question needs to be, Now that I get some of this character stuff, what can I learn from my present situation? It is only a slightly different question, but it gets your mind focused in on searching for the right answers, the answers that will polish your character. You may raise doubts with your questions. It is okay to have some doubts while you work on yourself. It means that you have something else to learn about yourself and reality.

Most of the time, though, rather than dealing with reality we decide to change location and change others. But as Emerson so aptly put it, "No change of circumstances can repair a defect of character."

Changing others is a trap too. It is focusing on the part you can't control hoping to make reality bend to your will. Reality doesn't change. You do. Let God deal with the flaws in others, and work on your own. That is the only way you can work with reality.

Working with reality. Reality is a strange concept. Everyone's view of it is different, and there are nearly six billion views. There is a way of approaching reality that will help you cash your character flaws in for wholesome qualities. I call it the reality response. It was developed for a couple of very cerebral addicts who couldn't understand change. They needed a diagram and a flow chart. One of them was a software engineer, so he had to see the connections in the mind in order to see how the reprogramming was done.

The reality response goes like this:

- Am I in reaction?
- Which character flaw or flaws are surfacing?
- What is the goofy belief that requires the use of that flaw?
- What need is it taking care of?
- Acknowledge that my flawless self doesn't have needs
- What is a new and better belief?
- Which virtue does the new belief require?
- Become willing to live that virtue

Am I in reaction? What a thought! It means using a character flaw as an automatic response to life. Could you possibly be in reaction to reality, using a character flaw where virtue would get better results? Of course you could. You know by now that your ego uses character flaws without asking your permission. So rather than white knuckle it, desperately trying to keep the flaws from surfacing, acknowledge that they are there. They will surface with or without your permission anyway, so observe them.

Which character flaw or flaws are surfacing? Once you start to identify which one has taken over your life for the moment, see if it is connected to any others. Often there is a cycle that we go through that links one flaw to another. Here is an example, I feel inadequate. Then I feel like a victim. I become intolerant of my victimizers and become raging indignant. Everybody has their own little clusters that they use on special occasions, like sunny days, rainy days, during daylight saving time, or at nighttime. It doesn't matter what happens to be the convenient excuse to use character flaws. We use them to protect our goofy beliefs.

What is the goofy belief that requires the use of that flaw? Everybody has some goofy beliefs. I hope by now you have accepted that premise. Our beliefs are in place to help us fulfill our deep needs of belonging, appreciation, freedom, and fun. When a flaw surfaces it is trying to see that your needs are met.

What need is it taking care of? Are you trying to get approval, belong, have fun, or get freedom? You feel a lack when you are using a flaw. But what if you didn't have that need? That's right. The character flaw would become dormant until the need surfaced again.

Acknowledge that your flawless self doesn't have needs. Here is a leap of faith for you. Suppose your flawless self is as I say it is. Then your inner core was the fulfillment of your needs all along. You didn't have to go anywhere or be anything to belong, to be free, to have fun or be appreciated. Your flawless self is appreciation, bliss, freedom, and belonging itself. You may as well get used to the idea, that's who you are regardless of what other stuff life has taught you. Your ego will deceive you and use flaws to protect you, but deep inside you know the truth. That is the only reality that is consistent in the six billion viewpoints out there. The view looks like this, "I am being, awareness, and bliss." The other stuff is fluff to make life interesting.

Since that's the way it really is, wouldn't it be better to let go of your goofy beliefs?

What is a new and better belief? Ask yourself to develop some other beliefs. You are going to have to play with this for a while to get the hang of it, but there is a key to doing it.

Which virtue does the new belief require? What is a new and better belief that will take care of the four needs but requires that I use a virtue instead of a flaw? Ask yourself that question. In it lies the key to creating new beliefs and developing great strength of character. The wholesome quality or the divine characteristic will typically be the virtue you lacked when you went into reaction. You see, this stuff is not really that complicated. In fact it is simple. The problem is that our whining egos need to be dragged along with us. Our egos are pessimistically forecasting disaster if we use virtues instead of flaws. Try it out. Use tolerance instead of intolerance today. Be willing to do it in spite of the doom and gloom that your ego throws at you.

Become willing to live that virtue! We are back to willingness. That's what makes this process so easy. If you had to use willpower to do it, you probably couldn't. But somewhere hidden inside is a wonderful spiritual gift that operates like this. Become willing and everything you need will arrive in due time. Be patient and stay willing.

That's the reality response in a nutshell. I could do a whole book on belief-change processes, but let's keep it simple.

Develop great beliefs that reflect great character. As long as you are changing your beliefs about your needs you may as well change your beliefs about yourself. The beliefs you have about your identity color every aspect of your life. Character transformation is associated with global identity belief change. By that I mean, when you change what you believe about your identity everything shifts. You get global change.

As you change, you start to believe that you have a mission or an overriding purpose in life. I call that your preeminent purpose. Mother Teresa once told me that she was a pencil in God's hands. That is an identity belief. It reflects her purpose. Develop a truly magnificent vision of yourself. Then you will be forced from the inside out to develop the character to match your vision.

You can change other beliefs that you carry around. Remember to doubt the old belief first and then retire it. Select a new belief and dwell on what it would mean if it were possible. Then see what virtues it requires you to develop.

Use virtues. It has been said that the dark side of one's personality may be closest to the light. Your strengths grow out of your weakness and your virtues grow out of the compost heap of your character flaws. Never choose to be discouraged when a flaw surfaces. Rejoice that you are just a few steps away from greater strength and virtue. Use your wholesome qualities every opportunity you can. They will strengthen gradually and almost imperceptibly until they are a habit. But you have to do something to keep the process going. As Saint Francis de Sales said centuries ago, "Now and then you must beat your wings to increase the altitude of your flight." Once the use of virtue becomes automatic, your flaws become harder to use.

Associate with those who show signs of character. This is the final stage in the development of character. It take good association to finish the job. We transform better in group than we do alone contemplating our navels. If that is your path, though, pursue it but don't get stuck on belly-button lint. Most of us need to be involved with others. This gives us the opportunity to make amends to others and to be examples for those just starting on the path.

There are a number of characteristic signs or marks of character that you will notice in others. Look for them in your friends and associates. Life will be more fulfilling.

THE SEVEN MARKS OF CHARACTER

• Surrender—the mark of greatness!

• Honesty—the mark of realism!

- Forgiveness—the mark of humility!
- Confidence—the mark of faith!
- Tolerance—the mark of perfection!
- Peacefulness—the mark of wisdom!
- Selfless service—the mark of love!

Surrender—the mark of greatness! You know individuals who live this principle. They are the humble few who, as Thoreau said, "walk consciously only partway toward our goal, and then leap in the dark to our success." They are fearless because the results are not what they are trying to control. They are working on bringing willingness to surrender into every situation. They are willing to surrender their egos to their flawless self, and in the process they receive a magnificent character makeover. Sure, it happens from the inside out and sometimes can't be seen easily. Sometimes those who are courageous enough to surrender to living a life of high values are ridiculed. It doesn't matter. Greatness can be found in one who is willing to change and willing to be all that he or she is capable of.

Surrender is the key to releasing flaws. When you are willing to use your God-given virtues in a difficult situation you have moved from the willfull use of character flaws to surrender.

Honesty—the mark of realism! Associate with honest individuals. It is so much easier to work with people who say what they mean and do what they say. Look for people who keep their promises. Avoid people who tell you what you want to hear and promise you anything as long as you will like them.

Honesty requires realism. Honesty embraces reality. Honesty protects you. The longer you practice it the easier life becomes. Base your associations on honesty and life will become almost effortless.

Forgiveness—the mark of humility! It is refreshing to associate with people who are truly humble. The humble don't grovel before the rich and powerful, nor do they shy away from the poor and downtrodden. The humble have made peace with everyone. They have made forgiveness a cornerstone of their character. They don't judge you lest they be judged themselves. They expect to be measured by the same standards that they use. Associating with others who practice forgiveness allows you to understand how this powerful spiritual principle functions as the great equalizer. My friend Wayne Dyer cleaned the slate with his father through forgiveness. It was a pivotal point in his remarkable career. People who are forgiving get to start with a clean slate with everyone, especially themselves.

When you work on character transformation you will repeatedly have to forgive yourself. Bring that mark of character to your relationships too.

Confidence—the mark of faith! You see it immediately. Faith marks you with confidence, not arrogance. Confidence is like a flag that some people wear. When it is based on self-esteem, great purpose in life, and comes with humility you know that the person is walking in faith. Avoid the arrogant. Walk with the confident.

Tolerance—the mark of acceptance! First of all, let me stress that having a pristine character means tolerance toward yourself and others. It is more important to be tolerant of other people's flaws than of your own. If you have gotten the overall picture, you know that you never have to be intolerant to process your flaws. The true mark of perfection comes when intolerance is not needed to motivate you to change.

When you associate with individuals who have arrived at this level of perfection, they are tolerant and loving to you despite your flaws. They are not, however, accepting of your flaws. They demand change but tolerate the fact that you may struggle with it. They demand that you work on your character. They are supportive of you even if you are getting blasted by the consequences of your flaws. They don't tolerate your flaws and make excuses. They are tolerant because they understand who you are, the flawless self.

Peacefulness—the mark of wisdom! A few very wise individuals have crossed my path. I am grateful to God for them. They have taught me that it is okay to be peaceful. They have been living ex-amples that life doesn't need to be lived from turmoil. When you see this type of individual, cherish the relationship. Hang on to it and nurture it as best you can.

My friend and mentor, the late Og Mandino, was one of these rare individuals. He was a wise man. He was peaceful most of the time. He was still passionate about life. You don't need to be a pansy or a pushover to be peaceful. You can be passionate about the things that matter to you. Og wasn't a gregarious guy. He was easygoing and sincere. His wisdom touched countless lives. He didn't motivate as a speaker. He was inspirational. Individuals with the mark of wis-dom will cross your path, especially in times of turmoil. They are a gift from God showing to you that there is a better way than being in reaction.

Selfless service—the mark of love! The final mark of great char-acter is the willingness to sacrifice for the sake of others without the expectation of anything in return. This is the mark of love. This is the purest expression of love that we can make to our fellow man. Associate with people who give of themselves selflessly and, better yet, anonymously. Love has no expectations, seeks no rewards, ex-pects no praise. Love is giving. Love is consistently selfless. Love shares because it exists to give itself away.

In a world like ours where everyone is after a piece of the pie and looking for fame, those marked by love know that the pie isn't theirs and that fame is an illusion. Love is its own reward.

Seek not only to associate with individuals with these marks of character but to be one yourself. Every situation is an opportunity for you to bring love, wisdom, and acceptance into it. You are the bearer of good news that life is splendid. Character can change. The rewards are great.

Sanity and Serenity

"What's in it for me?" I have been asked that question repeatedly when my clients have realized that the change begins with them. It is tough to quantify what is really in store for them. I often thought of having members of groups that were finishing come in and tell the groups that were starting where they would be going. I didn't have to. My schedule forced me to do two groups a night. They were generally late evening and the patients compared notes. The ones who were near the end of the program were selling the new ones on persisting.

"What's in it for you is sanity and serenity," one of my patients told an anxious group waiting for me one night when I was running late.

"What's that supposed to mean?" asked one of the more skeptical beginners.

The answer was simple but filled with wisdom. "Sanity is allowing God to turn you into you the thing you think you lack the most. Like if you need peace of mind you become peacefulness. And serenity is accepting the fact that it's true." She gave me a smile as I entered that said, "I don't believe this stuff, I know it."

My advice to you is to practice working on your character flaws until you understand her statement. You can have sanity, whatever that is for you, and you can be serene. I don't mean out in lala land unable to function, but living up to your full potential with willingness, initiative, courage, and love.

You Know You Are Making Progress!

When you start to use a character flaw, get annoyed and stop. That's right. You actually stop the anger and get curious to see what's going on inside. You know you've changed when people's flaws become a plea for love and acceptance. You no longer enable, but you no longer punish unjustly.

You're making progress when you no longer run around battered and abused looking for flaws in everyone else too. You know you're making progress when you're patient with beginners on the path but prudent with yourself. You know you're making progress when a flaw is just your ego asking your flawless self for a virtue, and you use one.

Shed Your Emotional Armor

The greatest protection you can give yourself is your character. It's not a bank account, fame, recognition, or intelligence, it is character that is life's true armor. All the emotional garbage we carry around trying to defend and protect ourselves is useless in the long run. Horace Greeley put it this way: "Fame is vapor, popularity an accident, riches take wings. Only one thing endures and that is character."

No matter what the starting point you have the ability to make great change if you are willing. You can shed your emotional armor because your flawless self is invincible to the petty arrows that bring down puffed-up egos.

Shed your emotional armor by fixing the old beliefs so that you function at your peak. Shed your emotional armor, because you no longer need the excuses that character flaws provide. Shed the dull armor of flaws and let your real character add sparkle to your life. It is as Aristotle said centuries ago, "Virtue, as well as evil, lies in our power and man is free to become whatever he envisions."

"The secret of success is constancy of purpose," said Benjamin Disraeli. Work on your flaws at every opportunity. Not through willpower, but through constant willingness. Always be willing to allow that great source of love and wisdom within you to give you what you need when you need it. Most of all be patient. As they say, God's not done with you yet. With God's grace and the ability to stay focused on high ideals you can change your character.

You started reading this book because there was something in your life that you wanted to change. You may have sensed that you wanted more out of relationships or maybe you wanted to know what to do with all the flawed people around you. Whatever your reason was for picking up this book, I suspect that you wanted to change how and where your life was going. You may have been looking for a tool to deal with a specific flaw. Some of you were even looking for something to dramatically impact your destiny. Here is the simple secret to remember: change your character and you will most definitely change your destiny.

In parting I leave you a small prayer.

May faith be the foundation of your talents,
may hope be the foundation of your dreams,
may love be the foundation of your character,
and may wisdom guide your passions.

Even if you doubt you can change, I'll be out there somewhere believing that you can.

A Flawless! Response to Reality

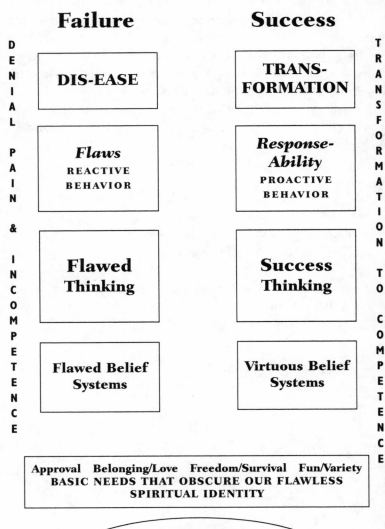

Failure **Success**

D
E
N
I
A
L

P
A
I
N

&

I
N
C
O
M
P
E
T
E
N
C
E

T
R
A
N
S
F
O
R
M
A
T
I
O
N

T
O

C
O
M
P
E
T
E
N
C
E

DIS-EASE **TRANS-FORMATION**

Flaws
REACTIVE
BEHAVIOR

Response-Ability
PROACTIVE
BEHAVIOR

Flawed Thinking **Success Thinking**

Flawed Belief Systems **Virtuous Belief Systems**

Approval Belonging/Love Freedom/Survival Fun/Variety
**BASIC NEEDS THAT OBSCURE OUR FLAWLESS
SPIRITUAL IDENTITY**

Soul **FLAWLESS** *Spirit*
—————
IDENTITY